INTERESTS AND THE
GROWTH OF KNOWLEDGE

BARRY BARNES
Science Studies Unit
University of Edinburgh

ROUTLEDGE DIRECT EDITIONS

Routledge & Kegan Paul
London, Boston and Henley

First published in 1977
by Routledge & Kegan Paul Ltd
39 Store Street,
London WC1E 7DD,
Broadway House,
Newtown Road,
Henley-on-Thames,
Oxon RG9 1EN and
9 Park Street,
Boston, Mass. 02108, USA
Reprinted in 1979
Printed in Great Britain by
Thomson Litho Ltd
East Kilbride, Scotland

British Library Cataloguing in Publication Data
Barnes, Barry
Interests and the growth of knowledge
1. Knowledge, Sociology of
I Title
301.2'1   BD175   77-30026

ISBN 0 7100 8669 5

CONTENTS

INTRODUCTION

This book is concerned with the study of general large scale
relationships between knowledge, social interests and social structure, and the problems which are generated thereby. Accordingly,
its focus is defined by a coherent tradition of writing in the
sociology of knowledge which includes work by Marx, Lukács, Weber,
Mannheim, Goldmann and Habermas, all of which is referred to and
utilised in the main text. For the sake of coherence the important work of Emile Durkheim and his followers is not discussed;
it comes close to providing an alternative tradition of thought
to that outlined above. Nor is there any extended discussion
of recent work on the negotiation of meanings and knowledge in
particular situations, although this material in the 'micro'
sociology of knowledge was of considerable utility in the development of the opinions which follow. I have judged it worth while,
for the sake of an orderly text, to make these restrictions of
scope, and consequently to advance some claims which are justified only via references, and which I hope to substantiate more
adequately in the future.
  There are two ways of expounding and utilising the work of a
group of authors such as that above. One is to embark upon a search
for what they 'really' meant, undertaking detailed analyses of
texts and sources, giving careful attention to matters of semantics
and problems of translation, examining in as much detail as possible the social situations wherein the works were produced, and,
not least, pointing out the particular interests and allegiances
of authors themselves and the way that they are reflected in their
writings. I possess neither the competences nor the interests
appropriate to this important form of analysis, and I shall not
attempt it here. There is, in any case, no lack of material of
this kind, and, with one or two of the authors mentioned above,
textual exegesis and associated historical research are flourish-
ing industries.
  The second possibility is to take the classic writings in the
sociology of knowledge as resources and sources of inspiration, in
formulating and dealing with problems of current interest and relevance. This is what is attempted here; hence the arrangement
of the book in terms of problems, rather than by author or chrono-

logy.   Sources and materials are invoked as they are required by
the context, rather than expounded for their own sake.   And the
emphasis is upon what existing work suggests, or how it can be
developed and extended, not upon what it denotes or what initially
it was a response to.   None the less, I have attempted to provide an adequate survey of the important themes in the relevant
part of the sociology of knowledge literature, and I am hopeful
that the result will serve as a textbook, to be read, as any such
text should be, in conjunction with the original works it discusses.

That there are few such texts available in the area of the sociology of knowledge was indeed one reason which led me to write this
book.   But there was also another, more significant, factor.
Work in the sociology of knowledge has predominantly been carried
out by politically active men, more familiar with political thought
than with any other kind.   Although they have often cited natural
scientific knowledge as their ideal model, they have rarely been
familiar with it, and have proceeded on the basis of their concrete familiarity with political thought, and perhaps some mis-
leading second-hand account of natural science.   My own competences and deficiences lie the other way entirely.   I was trained as
a natural scientist, and have been studying scientific knowledge
from a sociological perspective for a number of years (cf. Barnes,
1974);   I have no such concrete familiarity with explicitly
political thought.   It seemed to me likely that an examination of
the problems of the sociology of knowledge from a standpoint which
was bound to contrast sharply with that of most of its practitioners might both be generally productive and a source of insight
for myself.   Emphatically, however, what follows is not a technical
discussion centred upon the properties of esoteric scientific
knowledge.   Nor does it seek to assert the value and distinctive-
ness of such knowledge, after the manner of a scientistic tract.
Admittedly, the experience of a scientific training can reveal how
ludicrously misconceived polemics against science from intellectuals and social theorists sometimes are.   But, equally, it can
give the lie to idealisations of science, and alleged demonstrations of the special status of its knowledge.   One of the points
which will be made in what follows is that all knowledge, scientific or otherwise, should stand symmetrically from the standpoint
of sociological enquiry.

As I see it, the unusual perspective from which the text was
written is manifested not so much in the materials with which it
deals, or the evaluations which it makes of them, as in the forms
of argument and explanations which it employs.   Throughout, these
are avowedly naturalistic, in the sense that the discourse of the
natural sciences can be said to be naturalistic.   It is, indeed,
precisely the naturalistic prejudice of the text which leads it to
assert the sociological equivalence of all forms of knowledge;
I know of no naturalistic argument which indicates the contrary.

There should be no need to defend this naturalistic prejudice.
All work must develop in the light of some set of given presuppositions, and the best that one can do is to acknowledge their
existence and proceed from them as consistently and faithfully as
one can.   Hopefully, what follows will thereby show that a

naturalistic approach leads to a coherent and not altogether
commonplace account of the problems of the sociology of knowledge,
which provides some useful comparisons with existing points of
view.   It is true that many of the writers to be discussed worked
against the very different background assumptions of German
philosophy and the Hegelian tradition.   But since their thought is
taken as a resource, and not as something to be reconstructed here,
this should not constitute a problem.   Indeed, the ensuing clash
of interests and presuppositions might be considered a worthwhile source of insight in itself.

ACKNOWLEDGMENTS

The present text has benefited greatly from comments and criticisms made of earlier drafts, and from many informal discussions of its general themes. Particular thanks are due to Donald MacKenzie and Steven Shapin, from whom I have learned much in the course of what has been, for me, extremely valuable collaborative work, and to David Bloor, with whom I have shared a long-standing interest in the sociology of knowledge. However, whereas my specific debt to these colleagues will be apparent from the text, that due to many others will not. Accordingly, I should like to express my gratitude here to all those friends, colleagues and ex-colleagues who have helped me so much with their particular criticisms, their general interest and support, and their tolerant reception of the vague and ill-formulated notions which were initially thrust upon them as the book was being worked out. Its inadequacies, for which the responsibility is entirely my own, would indubitably have been more numerous and severe without them. I should also like to thank those members of the staff of the Science Studies Unit who helped to prepare the manuscript, and particularly Jane Haldane who undertook most of the typing.

Chapter 1

THE PROBLEM OF KNOWLEDGE

1 CONCEPTIONS OF KNOWLEDGE

An immediate difficulty which faces any discussion of the present
kind is that there are so many different conceptions of the nature
of knowledge. Some of these can be set aside, for sociological
purposes, by taking knowledge to consist in accepted belief, and
publicly available, shared representations. The sociologist is
concerned with the naturalistic understanding of what people take
to be knowledge, and not with the evaluative assessment of what
deserves so to be taken; his orientation is normally distinct from
that of the philosopher or epistemologist. But this still leaves
a daunting number of alternative conceptions of knowledge, and
how it is related to thought and activity on the one hand, and the
external world on the other. Although detailed consideration of
all these possibilities is out of the question, some such conception, however loose and informal, is essential if we are to
proceed. Perhaps the best compromise is briefly to examine two
general accounts of knowledge which have been of some sociological
significance, and to advocate a working conception developed from
one of them. This will involve setting aside many issues, and
almost entirely ignoring the important question of how people
learn. Hopefully, however, it will be found acceptable as a mode
of presentation, rather than a justification, of the position
advanced, and a setting of the scene for later, more concrete
discussion.

One common conception of knowledge represents it as the product
of contemplation. According to this account, knowledge is best
achieved by disinterested individuals, passively perceiving some
aspect of reality, and generating verbal descriptions to correspond
to it. Such descriptions, where valid, match reality, rather as
a picture may match in appearance some aspect of the reality it
is designed to represent. Invalid descriptions, on the other hand,
distort reality and fail to show a correspondence when compared
with it; often they are the products of social interests which
make it advantageous to misrepresent reality, or social restrictions upon the investigation of reality which make accurate perception of it impossible.

This contemplative account, as it can be called, unites a number of notions. It describes knowledge as the product of isolated individuals. And it assumes that the individuals intrude minimally between reality and its representation: they apprehend reality *passively,* and, as it were, let it speak for itself; their perception is independent of their interests, their expectations or their previous experience. Hence the knowledge they produce is essentially only a function of reality itself. It can be tested by any individual who is able to compare it with reality, since its property of correspondence with reality is entirely independent of the situation wherein it was produced. These various notions tend to be associated because they are all indicated by a simple, memorable, concrete model: learning and knowledge generation are thought of in terms of visual apprehension, and verbal knowledge by analogy with pictorial representation. Indeed, it is probably our intuitive sense of correspondence between a picture and the appearance of something real, which sustains much of the credibility of the contemplative account, at least at the everyday level.

Certainly, our everyday epistemological notions appear to be thoroughly permeated with this conception, and the analogy between learning and passive visual apprehension. We talk of understanding as 'seeing', or 'seeing clearly'; we are happy to talk of valid descriptions giving us a 'true picture'. Similarly, we are able to characterise inadequate knowledge as 'coloured', 'distorted', 'blind to relevant facts', and so on. The overall visual metaphor is a resource with which we produce accounts of the generation and character of truth and error. And in many ways these accounts serve us well. Nonetheless, in sociology, the contemplative account has always co-existed with a sharply contrasted alternative, and at the present time it is the latter toward which the general trend of thought is moving. Increasingly, knowledge is being treated as essentially social, as a part of the culture which is transmitted from generation to generation, and as something which is actively developed and modified in response to practical contingencies.

Such a conception stands in polar opposition to most of the elements of the contemplative account. Knowledge is not produced by passively perceiving individuals, but by interacting social groups engaged in particular activities. And it is evaluated communally and not by isolated individual judgments. Its generation cannot be understood in terms of psychology, but must be accounted for by reference to the social and cultural context in which it arises. Its maintenance is not just a matter of how it relates to reality, but also of how it relates to the objectives and interests a society possesses by virtue of its historical development. An appropriate concrete model which integrates these various themes can be provided by considering a society's knowledge as analogous to its techniques or its conventional forms of artistic expression, both of which are readily understood as culturally transmitted, and as capable of modification and development to suit particular requirements.

The relationship of these two opposed conceptions has always been an uneasy one within the context of sociology, with the

tension between the two always apparent, but with individual
writers rarely situating themselves consistently and unambiguously
on one side or the other. Thus, Karl Mannheim's 'Ideology and
Utopia' (1936) opens with a clear indication of its commitment to
the second, active conception:

> Strictly speaking it is incorrect to say that the single indi-
> vidual thinks. Rather it is more correct to insist that he
> participates in thinking further what other men have thought
> before him. He finds himself in an inherited situation with
> patterns of thought which are appropriate to this situation and
> attempts to elaborate further the inherited modes of response
> or to substitute others for them in order to deal more adequately
> with the new challenges which have arisen out of the shifts and
> changes in his situation. (Chapter 1.1)

But, although these points are reasserted a number of times
throughout the work, a great part of its argument and much of its
concrete discussion is, in fact, predicated upon the contemplative
model. Natural science and mathematics, Mannheim tells us, are
forms of knowledge which bear no mark of the context of their production and which can properly be assessed entirely in terms of
their correspondence with reality. Moreover, precisely *because*
they are the products of disinterested contemplation, they are
preferable to other kinds of knowledge, to sociology or history
or political thought.

In his treatment of these latter kinds of knowledge Mannheim
continues to be inconsistent. Sometimes he insists that this
knowledge can in no way be assessed in context-independent, contemplative terms. Then he develops an argument which implies the
opposite. He states that such knowledge, knowledge of social
reality, is always in practice related to social standpoints and
interests, and thus context-dependent. This makes the knowledge
inadequate or, at best, of restricted validity. However, under
ideal but realisable conditions, context-independent knowledge,
corresponding to social reality, could be produced. A class of
disinterested intellectuals, able to take a properly contemplative approach could produce it.

It is true that some of this inconsistency is the product of
Mannheim's combining essays written at different times. Chapters
1 and 5 are those most inclined to an active, contextual and
social treatment of knowledge, and they were the last written.
But these are also the least concrete chapters of the book. And
even in these chapters, the contemplative account and its associated
metaphors remain important components, without which the results
of Mannheim's thinking would be bereft of all plausibility and
coherence. It is clear that in spite of himself, Mannheim produced a work largely based upon the contemplative account.
Although he explicitly rejected it, he apparently could not help
but think in terms of it. Even the most original and insightful points in 'Ideology and Utopia' are conceptualised in terms
of contemplation, and the associated visual metaphors. (1)

Thus, Mannheim's work reveals just how difficult it can be to
move away from a contemplative position. The associated pictorial
metaphor for knowledge is so pervasive, intuitively attractive
and, indeed, valuable as an explanatory resource, that it can be

difficult in practice to structure one's thought independently of
it.   Mannheim knew, and advanced, many good arguments against the
contemplative account, and in favour of the alternative he explicitly advocated, but this did not suffice to reorient his practical approach.   Hence, given that a form of the active, social conception of knowledge is to be put forward as a working orientation
here, it seems appropriate to present it in a way which is designed
to counteract the appeal of the pictorial metaphors incorporated
in the contemplative account.   Such a presentation cannot hope
to count in any way as a justification;   it merely offers a model
for consideration, and for use in following the subsequent discussion.   But there is in any case no space in which to develop
a detailed discussion of the problems involved.

It might be thought that the best procedure for moving away from
the contemplative account would be to break the equivalence of
pictorial and verbal representations and emphasise the differences
between passive-visual apprehension and understanding generally.   If verbal statements cannot be matched against reality like
pictures are, then the need for an alternative metaphor to characterise the nature of verbal knowledge is indicated.   In fact, the
opposite strategy is the more expedient.   We should emphasise the
equivalence of all representations, pictorial or verbal, and accept
observing as a typical kind of learning.   It is the treatment of
visualisation and depiction as *passive* processes which marrs contemplative conceptions in the sociology of knowledge, and makes
their visual and pictorial metaphors unsatisfactory.   Our strategy
should be to reveal pictorial representation, the most favourable
case for the contemplative conception, as essentially an active
and a socially mediated process, and in this respect typical of
representation and knowledge generation generally.

In fact, this is something that has been done for us already by
those academic fields directly concerned with the study of pictorial
representations and their creation.   Work in fields as different
as the psychology of perception and the history of art could be
used to make the points we need.   Let us take the latter field,
where the close relationship, if not the complete equivalence, of
pictorial and verbal representation is more or less taken for
granted, and references to the 'language' or 'vocabulary' of an
artist or illustrator are commonplace.   A particularly relevant
work is that of Ivins (1953) on the history of prints and engrav-
ings.   Here language is looked to as a model on the basis of which
to understand pictures.   Ivins devotes his extremely concrete
and well-illustrated book to showing how the 'syntax' of 'pictorial
statements' has changed from the Renaissance to the present day.
And he makes it clear that the 'pictorial statements' he considers
simply cannot be treated as passive reflections of real appearances;   rather they render scenes and objects in terms of conventions.

Gombrich's important study 'Art and Illusion' (1959) makes
similar points.   It reveals the difficulties which arise in talking of the extent to which a representation can correspond to reality
or the direct appearance of reality.   And it makes clear that, at
least for intuitively straightforward conceptions of correspondence,
representations not only do not correspond with appearances but they

cannot (not even if they are photographs). Representations may, when viewed under particular conditions in particular contexts, achieve a 'trompe l'oeil', but such deceptions are generally produced by conventions of representation which involve obvious distortions of what the painter or illustrator sees. The capacity to produce 'realistic' representations tends to depend upon the study of existing paintings which use appropriate conventions, rather than upon an open observant attitude to what is depicted.

In Gombrich, Ivins and similar work, we find an account of the construction of pictorial representations which serves admirably as an informal working model for the construction of knowledge. Pictorial representations are actively constructed from conventions available as the resources of some culture or sub-culture. The successful realisation of paintings, for example, depends upon familiarity with existing paintings and illustrations and the conventions implicit in them. Such conventions are meaningful as words are meaningful, and are actively manipulated and organised in the light of particular aims or interests.

Extending this account, when a representation conveys knowledge or information about, say, an object, it is by classifying it, by making it an instance of one or more kinds of entity recognised by the culture whose resources are drawn upon. In this way the representation makes it possible for existing knowledge to be applied to its referent, and it makes the referent a source of meaningful information, a potential check upon existing knowledge. Knowledge and object are connected by the representation. (We can, admittedly, deploy knowledge directly as we act, but this is because our perception organises and pre-classifies what we perceive; we read the world, rather as we read handwriting, as an assemblage of symbols.) (2)

All representations are indeed then, as Ivins says, kinds of statement. They must be distinguished both from the objects they represent and from the appearances of those objects. Any representation is one of numerous possibilities which the resources of a culture make available. And the resources of a culture are themselves reasonably treated as a particular selection from an endless number of possibilities. In both cases, we are entitled to seek an explanation of why some possibilities rather than others are actually encountered.

It may well be that particular individuals frequently notice resemblances between aspects of their environment in a random, undirected way, and build up particular beliefs and representations in a fashion which cannot be explained systematically. But public knowledge typically evolves much more coherently, and the people who contribute representations to it operate in what is cumulatively a much more orderly way. Typically they are concerned, directly or indirectly, in the performance of some institutionalised activity, designed to further particular aims or ends. This means that the knowledge they produce is designed from the start to facilitate certain kinds of prediction, or function in the performance of particular kinds of competence. And its evaluation is pre-structured to an extent by these design requirements; to anticipate Habermas's term, discussed in the next section, it is pre-structured by a situated technical 'interest in prediction and control'.

Representations are not assessed with any particular stress on
their rendering of appearances, but instrumentally, in conjunction
with whatever the activities are with which they function. Hence,
the growth of knowledge should not be thought of as the result of
random learning about reality, but as the correlate of the historical development of procedures, competences and techniques
relevant in various degrees to the ends or objectives of cultures
or sub-cultures. Of course, many such competences and associated
representations find such wide instrumental applicability that
once introduced into practically any culture they are almost
guaranteed an enduring position therein.

Representations are actively manufactured renderings of their
referents, produced from available cultural resources. The particular forms of construction adopted reflect the predictive or
other technical cognitive functions the representation is required to perform when procedures are carried out, competences
executed, or techniques applied. Why such functions are initially required of the representation is generally intelligible,
directly or indirectly, in terms of the objectives of some social
group.

This very informal conception should suffice as a basis for
the following discussion, although for many purposes it would
be altogether inadequate as it stood. It would need considerable
qualification, for example, if activities like scientific research were the central foci of discussion, with their basic
orientation to the creative extension of knowledge. It is often
pointed out that theories and representations employed for creative
scientific work are often not those which have proved the most
instrumentally adequate. Scientists often impute instrumental
adequacy to one set of representations (say those of classical
mechanics or geometrical optics) but regard others, those they
use in their work, as having greater ontological adequacy. This
is often taken to indicate that knowledge must be, and is,
evaluated as a direct rendering of reality and not simply as an
aid to activity. Unfortunately yesterday's ontologies have a
depressing tendency to become tomorrow's instrumentally adequate
representations, and on that basis, and other grounds which cannot be gone into here, the general outlines of the present account can be adequately defended. Nonetheless, the actors' distinction between instrumentally applicable theories and those
suitable as guides to research is of great relevance and interest,
and would merit extended discussion in other contexts. (3)

Let us however concentrate on our informal conception as it
stands, and try to make it a little more concrete by reference
to some examples. In order to continue to erode the appeal of a
contemplative conception of knowledge, pictorial representations
will be used. And so that the representations will be generally
accepted as embodying knowledge, the illustrations chosen will
be of a kind which have utility in the context of natural
science. They will be considered in order, from those which are
easily reconciled with the above account, to those which may not
immediately appear to be so. Hopefully, the sequence will act as
a 'bridge' to the most problematic cases, and indicate the fully
general scope of the account.

   Imagine then that some students in a physics laboratory are
requested to draw some appartus set out before them, and that the
result is Figure 1.1;   such a result is not empirically unreason-
able.   Presumably, there is no problem in arguing that the figure
is a pictorial statement constructed from existing cultural resources;   it is assembled from signs meaningful as concepts in
physical theories of electricity, and is obviously reminiscent

Figure 1.1

of a verbal statement.   Perhaps the commonest immediate concern
of students who construct diagrams like Figure 1.1 is to conform
to expectations, but basically such representations are sustained
in our culture as adjuncts to competences.   In this case, it
scarcely makes sense to ask whether the referent of Figure   1.1
is truly what the figure indicates it to be: the referent could
be a battery and a resistance box wired together, a length of metal,
a nerve fibre, a building or indeed practically anything at all.
The appropriateness of the figure cannot be assessed in isola-
tion, by examination of its referent.   All that can be assessed
is the use of the figure, how it is actively employed.
   The real problem with Figure 1.1 is likely to lie in establishing that it is a typical representation.   In particular,
there is no vestige of resemblance between its appearance and that
of what it is used to represent.   Let us move then to Figure 1.2.
Maps frequently show an intuitive resemblance to the appearance
of reality itself, as, for example, when it is seen from the air;
sometimes they are deliberately designed to resemble appearances.
But they remain compatible with the above account.   They are constructed entirely in terms of conventions.   Their particular
form depends upon what procedures they are designed to facilitate.
Their value is assessed functionally and not by reference to
appearance.   Maps indeed afford one of the clearest and most
accessible contexts in which to examine the connection between
the structure of representations and their function.   (If ever
physics needs to be supplemented as a paradigm of knowledge, there
is much to be said for turning to cartography.)
   Figure 1.3 is taken from an anatomy textbook, and depicts some
muscles of 'the arm'.   It is designed to facilitate recognition
and naming in the context of an esoteric activity.   *Therefore,* it
is not a rendering of a particular arm.   Despite being apparently
realistic it is intentionally a schemata.   It cannot be taken as
an attempt passively to imitate reality.   Indeed its effect is to
modify perception so that students can perceive arms in terms of
its scheme of representation.   As an aid to seeing and naming,

Figure 1.2

its schematic character is accentuated at the expense of its
possibilities as a rendition of appearances. There is no particular arm to which it relates as a representation; it is a typi-
fication constructed from available symbols. (That it is indeed
constructed from symbols can only escape our notice if we forget
that symbols are involved in *perception* as well as representation.)

Like all scientific representations, Figure 1.3 is reliably
applicable only to aid particular kinds of procedure. In this
case the procedures, together with directly associated instrumental interests, are embodied in the role of the anatomist
and his student audience. Those who make practical use of such
representations are generally well aware that their reliability
and applicability is restricted; this awareness is automatically
generated in learning to use the representations. Other instrumental interests and other activities, located in other scientific roles, engender other kinds of representation. But this
limitation upon the scope of anatomical representations is not
normally taken as grounds for scepticism about their validity;

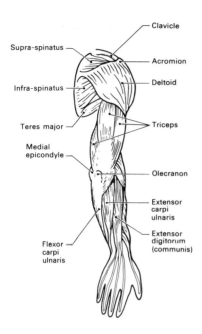

Figure 1.3

they are accepted and accorded credibility co-extensively with
the acceptance of anatomists' competences and techniques.

When representations are photographs and not diagrammatic
figures, the same interpretation applies. Such photographs remain
constructs for use in activity. Admittedly, the photographer cannot simply assemble conventional symbols when he takes a photo-
graph of some real object. But he can work his material so that
his finished product can be seen in terms of, or *as*, such an
assemblage. (4) Examination of the photographs sometimes used
in the teaching of human anatomy illustrates this point convincingly. Their manufacture does, of course, involve the use of
particular human bodies, but their representational adequacy is
again evaluated in use, and not by comparing them with the particular bodies from which they were manufactured.

The argument is then that all representations, pictorial or
verbal, realistic or abstract, are actively constructed assemblages of conventions or meaningful cultural resources, to be understood and assessed in terms of their role in activity. (5)
Essentially this amounts to making representations analogous to
techniques, artistic conventions or other typical forms of culture,
rather than considering them in terms of the contemplative conception. Sociologists have often found it appropriate to adopt
this treatment in dealing with everyday knowledge. But, like
Mannheim, they have sometimes felt that a special kind of knowledge exists in the natural sciences and mathematics, intelligible
only in contemplative terms. Scientific knowledge, however, is
always assessed in conjunction with the institutionalised
technical procedures of its specialities and is entirely typical

of knowledge in general: science is in many ways a constellation of craft skills. (6)   As for mathematical knowledge, we have
here a developed set of generally utilisable procedures and
representations to which no reality can even be said to correspond. (7)   It is precisely their extraordinary versatility in
furthering a vast range of objectives, which results in their
widespread use and sustains their credibility as knowledge.

However, in thus rejecting a contemplative conception of knowledge and adopting a view which emphasises its social dimension,
it is important not to lose sight of the connection which does
exist between knowledge and the real world.   This is properly
stressed in the contemplative account, albeit usually in terms of
an unclear notion of truth as correspondence.   Knowledge is not
related to activity rather than reality;   it is related to activity
which consists precisely in men attempting to manipulate, predict
and control the real world in which they exist.   Hence knowledge
is found useful precisely because the world is as it is;   and it
is to that extent a function of what is real, and not the pure
product of thought and imagination.   Knowledge arises out of our
encounters with reality and is continually subject to feedback-
correction from these encounters, as failures of prediction
manipulation and control occur.   We seek to eliminate such
failures, but so far reality has sustained its capacity to surprise us and dash our expectations.   Indeed, our liability to be
surprised in this way, to be confounded in our expectations, constitutes an important argument against a purely idealist theory
of knowledge.   (8)

2 KNOWLEDGE AND INTERESTS

Many important insights into how our knowledge of reality is
mediated by interests and activity are to be found in Marx's
work.   They have been taken up by European writers on what might
loosely be called the idealist wing of Marxism, and incorporated
into general theories of knowledge which offer a striking contrast with the predominant conceptions in our own academic
culture.   These conceptions, a strict separation of fact and value,
a stress on the objects of knowledge almost to the extent of
excluding the role of the knowing subject, a view of that subject
as an isolated contemplative individual without social dimensions
or historical situation, and an atomistic concept of validation
which sets isolated bits of knowledge in comparison with individual fragments of reality, are all condemned under the somewhat confusing umbrella label of 'positivism'.   They must be swept
aside, it is claimed, and replaced by a more down-to-earth
account which treats knowledge as the actual product of men as
they live and work in society.

Clearly, work which develops such important themes as these
is of great importance and must be examined.   Paradoxically,
however, one of its most characteristic features is its lack of
contact with actual instances of knowledge in its social context.
That intimate involvement with the specifics of concrete historical situations, so laudable in Marx's work, and, one would

have thought, an implied necessity in terms of their own theories, is generally absent from the writings of the idealist Marxists, where, with few exceptions, one finds only large-scale speculations. There is no doubt that the work to be dicussed here has suffered as a consequence. The theories of Lukács and Habermas both involve weaknesses which attention to concrete examples would have exposed and helped to eliminate.

Lukács set out his views in his famous polemic 'History and Class-Consciousness' (1923). Here he contemptuously rejected contemplative positions and asserted that consciousness and thus knowledge, of all kinds, in all contexts, was necessarily related to human interests; it was always the product of the activity of particular groups of men, rationally generating it in the course of furthering their interests. (9)   Indeed, for Lukács, men's rationality was manifest not in their thinking alone, but in their thought and activity considered as one phenomenon, that is, in their practice. Unlike Mannheim, whose work he directly inspired, Lukács consistently stressed the need to consider practice, rather than thought alone, whenever knowledge and consciousness were under sociological investigation. In this he was entirely justified. What is open to question is whether even Lukács's work takes sufficient account of the man-created character of knowledge.

Lukács believed that under ideal conditions reality is fully accessible to the rational appraisal of men; the totality of what is real can potentially be understood. Men generate knowledge in the course of practice, to further their particular interests. Were practice unconstrained, the totality of these interests would amount to the universal, fully general, interests of mankind as a whole, and would generate the fullest possible understanding of reality. But in existing societies, practice is never unconstrained. That of oppressed classes is restricted by coercion and by ideological control. And that of dominant social classes is ultimately restricted by their own particular, restricted social interests, which limit the possible scope of their rationality. Awareness of some aspects of reality is irrelevant, or in some cases positively discomforting to them, and consequently is not developed; thus they never attain more than a partial understanding of reality. Moreover, there is a sense in which this partial understanding is a total misunderstanding. We can only properly understand an aspect of reality by considering it in context, in relation to everything else; hence to understand anything fully and correctly we must understand everything. It follows that the particular restricted interests of a class set limits upon the whole of its thinking, and *logically determine* the most that it can hope to produce in the way of knowledge. To every class there corresponds an ideal class-consciousness. (10)

Without in any way addressing the problematic question of what Lukács's own views were on the subject, it is worth noting that his account is readily intelligible if we assume that the knowledge which men generate in the course of their practice is in some sense a copy, reflection or picture of an aspect of reality. This assumption justifies the notion of a full and final under-

standing of reality as a whole. It allows us to conceive of
'partial consciousness' in terms of actors having access only to
parts of a complete picture of something. And it suggests that
the missing pieces of the picture will be aspects of the whole
irrelevant or disquieting to a particular class, and hence not
reflected in its consciousness. If we do not make this assumption then it is difficult to see how to integrate and justify
the various themes of Lukács's argument, or how to interpret a
number of other points in his work. (11)   Perhaps pictorial metaphors did, at some level, help to structure even Lukács's thought.

In any case, among its many weaknesses, Lukács's position
overlooks or ignores the fact that men's thinking is always an
extension of earlier thought, that the production of new knowledge
involves the use of existing knowledge and existing cultural resources, and that consciousness is to this extent always the product
of history. It assumes instead an unproblematic interaction between men and reality, with a third variable, interest, effectively
doing no more than accounting for the restricted scope of that
interaction. Once it is realised that, as Lukács might have said,
new knowledge is dialectically generated from old, then the
entire structure of his account falls to pieces. Knowledge has
to be understood naturalistically in terms of its cultural antecedents and its present causes, not teleologically in terms of a
future state it is or is not moving towards. An ideal 'complete'
state of knowledge, a complete understanding of reality, can no
longer be assumed; it is indeed no longer clear what the meaning
of such a conception can be. And, accordingly, interest can no
longer determine consciousness by restricting it to involvement with
some section of the whole of reality.

Like Mannheim, Lukács made promising programmatic statements
about the general character of consciousness, and failed to develop
them into a satisfactory framework for the sociology of knowledge. His failure is however differently rooted to that of
Mannheim. Lukács seems to have lacked any real curiosity about
knowledge and consciousness, and to have written largely to legitimate projected courses of action. He disdained to consider concrete instances, and thus was incapable of learning; his thinking
was cut off from dialectical interaction with experienced reality.

The work of Jurgen Habermas has many of the weaknesses of
Lukács's, and for similar reasons. Nonetheless, his 'Knowledge
and Human Interests' (1972) is a significant text, which, although
only fully intelligible in terms of an intellectual tradition
entirely alien to that in which this book must reside, can still
be exploited as a source of particular insights. (12)   Let us
start by outlining his conception of modern scientific knowledge,
which he takes as the predominant current form of technical, instrumentally oriented knowledge, and typical of such knowledge.

Habermas sees scientific knowledge as the product of communities
of interacting men who operate upon and perceive reality, not
idly and contemplatively, but in terms of particular instrumental,
manipulative and predictive interests. Such interests are constituted into the process of knowledge generation and evaluation.
What scientists *mean* by the validity of their knowledge is predetermined by these interests. What scientists take to be facts

or data is determined by the pragmatic pre-organisation of experience implied by existing systems of instrumental activity. (13)
Scientific knowledge has a function only in the context of systems
of instrumental activity.

Since particular areas of scientific knowledge are bound up
with systems of instrumental action, they relate to each other just
as our instrumental activities relate to each other: they constitute an overall body of knowledge available in the execution of
goal-oriented, instrumental action, a general interpretation of
reality with a view to all possible forms of technical control and
prediction. According to Habermas, scientific knowledge, and
technical knowledge generally, is oriented, with transcendental
necessity, by a *knowledge constitutive interest* (KCI) in prediction and control; this interest is the natural basis for scientific knowledge. And far from this reflecting adversely upon the
worth of science, it is, for Habermas, the source of its justification: modern science is to be valued in that it is the most
developed form of instrumentally oriented knowledge.

Essentially, the tendency to treat interest as an adverse influence upon knowledge, and to represent science as the product of
disinterested contemplation, stems from a justified distrust of
the effects of particular narrow individual and social interests,
which generate rationalisations and ideology. All scientific dis-
ciplines correctly guard themselves against such interests. But
this has led to an incorrect understanding of the general
relationship of knowledge and interest:

> Because science must secure the objectivity of its statements
> against the pressure and seduction of particular interests, it
> deludes itself about the fundamental interests to which it owes
> not only its impetus but *the conditions of possible objectivity*
> themselves. (p. 311)

Whether or not this diagnosis is correct, Habermas's assertion
of the necessary connection of scientific knowledge and technical
interests, and his consequent instrumentalist account of science,
are probably, in general terms, justified. (14) It is true that
they involve difficulties and obscurities, and that his discussion
of 'transcendental' KCIs is particularly tentative and unsatisfactory. (15) But most of these problems are more pertinent to
grand speculative philosophy than to the vulgar naturalistic
concerns of the present volume, where we can simply take the point
that technical and scientific knowledge is generated and evaluated out of an active interest in prediction and control.

Unfortunately, the remaining themes in Habermas's discussion of
knowledge are worth attention primarily because of the plausible but
disastrous misconceptions which they involve. Science, we are
told, is the best we can achieve in the way of instrumental knowledge; but men have other interests besides instrumental ones,
and knowledge can be constituted in relation to these interests
also. Moreover, such knowledge can exist in institutionalised
forms, with their own agreed standards of validity, fully on a par
with the institutionalised forms of scientific knowledge.
Habermas is not calling our attention to such things as our personal memories with their emotional or aesthetic meanings. Nor
is he reminding us that our knowledge may be modulated, at the

public level, by the desire for self-consolation or the aim of deceiving others; as we have seen, he accepts that particular interests of this kind should be prevented from influencing the processes of knowledge generation. He is suggesting that further ideal conceptions of knowledge must be accepted, every bit as important as the scientific-instrumental ideal, but relating to other KCIs.

Habermas offers us two further such ideals, related to two further distinct KCIs (pp. 308-11): historical-hermeneutic knowledge relates to a *practical* KCI in meaningful communication and the achievement of consensus; (16) knowledge involving self-reflection (as in philosophy and 'critical' sciences) arises out of an *emancipatory* KCI in autonomy and responsibility. (17) Consideration of the former ideal will suffice to illustrate the problems he thereby creates. Habermas claims that the evalua-tion of, for example, historical knowledge is structured by interests different to those operative in the case of science, and that the knowledge itself is intrinsically different in charac-ter from scientific knowledge. He fails to substantiate his first claim due to inadequate consideration of the nature of historical knowledge (or 'hermeneutic' knowledge generally); he errs in his second claim due to his inadequate familiarity with scientific knowledge. He is correct in maintaining that men possess diverse interests, and that their consciousness is not entirely dominated by the instrumental aims of prediction and control. But his specific equation of different kinds of interest with different kinds of knowledge does not stand up to detailed consideration.

According to Habermas, whereas science is evaluated by the extent to which it facilitates instrumental operations with things, historical knowledge is evaluated by success in the 'preserva-tion and expansion of the intersubjectivity of possible action-orienting mutual understanding' (p. 310). It is the kind of knowledge in terms of which people achieve identity and self-integration, and in terms of which they interact with others to achieve an 'unconstrained consensus'. Unfortunately, we are pro-vided with no satisfactory concrete exemplification of this abstract statement, nor any other relevant indication of how *precisely* interests in interaction and consensus structure the evaluation of historical knowledge. Nor is it easy to imagine what Habermas has in mind.

It is inconceivable that history should be treated as purely expedient myth or fable, constructed solely with a view to what an audience wants to hear, or what would best serve the cause of social solidarity. Conceptions of what actually happened and what factors were relevant to men's actions, are obviously of great importance in history, together with scholarly methods of inferring such things from sources and records. Indeed, who would argue that such concerns should not take priority over any other considerations, when historical accounts are being evalu-ated? Certainly Habermas gives no indication of such scant regard for scholarly historical standards, and never anywhere suggests that they should be set aside out of expediency.

Yet, if the framework of evaluation of historical knowledge is primarily defined by these considerations, rather than by expedient considerations, it is very difficult to see why that framework should primarily be related to a KCI in dialogue and consensus. It would seem rather to be analogous to the evaluative framework of science. Doubtless, there are ways of countering this objection. It might be said, for example, that we should consider the evaluation of *concepts* in science and history, not of statements, or actual knowledge claims: whereas the prior evaluation of scientific concepts is instrumentally informed, the prior evaluation of historical concepts and their meanings is informed by their potential in the maintenance of dialogue and the attainment of consensus. (18) This is a possibility that deserves exploration, but, again, it is impossible to discern what it might involve from consideration of Habermas's work. How we rationally evaluate concepts and meanings in a way which reflects a prior interest in dialogue and consensus is unclear. It is no less problematic a notion than that of the evaluation of actual knowledge claims in terms of the same interest. Habermas simply does not satisfactorily justify and illustrate his point of view here.

Admittedly, the character of historical knowledge and how it compares with the knowledge of science is an extraordinarily difficult question. But let us for the sake of a clear discussion move right to the opposite pole to Habermas, and hold that historical knowledge is instrumental in just the same way as is scientific knowledge. To the extent that historians prefer the evidence of their sources to the requirements of their community or their audience, they are surely operating in terms of an interest in prediction and control rather than in consensus. Their findings are properly thought of as predictions of subsequent archaeological or paleological discoveries; their reconstructions of the past may constitute virtual experiments on the basis of which to learn how to predict, or even influence, the course of social change.

Historians, we might suggest, typically and properly evaluate their knowledge (and their concepts) in a framework pre-structured by interests in prediction or control, even if often with a view to using it to serve a variety of further interests. It may *then* assist individuals to orient themselves within their communities, or it may facilitate predictions of social or even individual behaviour. On this view, history differs from science not by virtue of the general interests which are constituted into the process of its production and evaluation, but by virtue of the interests it typically serves and the subject matter out of which it arises. Thus,there is a strong case for treating historical knowledge as *primarily* instrumental in character; it is not perhaps entirely analogous to physics or mechanical engineering knowledge, but is fully comparable with say palaeontology, or other sciences where immediate manipulative interests are not relevant, but the characteristic general cognitive operations involved in prediction and control are nonetheless manifest.

Along the same lines, it could be argued that *all* knowledge, 'scientific', 'hermeneutic' or otherwise, is primarily produced and evaluated in terms of an interest in prediction and control. We further our interest in communication and mutual understanding

on the basis of *any* body of shared knowledge, which we make the
basis of interaction by utilising *communicative competences*.
Consensus in a community is not achieved by the application of a
particular kind of public knowledge, but by the exercise of communicative skills and proclivities against the background of
whatever it is in the way of knowledge that members of the community
generally possess. Such skills and proclivities are currently the
subject of study by some 'ethnomethodologists' and 'cognitive
sociologists'. By their use we achieve an everyday consensus on
the basis of what is accounted the common sense of our culture;
historians achieve a consensus on the basis of their esoteric
findings; and scientists achieve a consensus in their esoteric
interactions on the basis of their theories and models. According to this view, knowledge has the character of a *resource,*
communally exploited in the achievement of whatever interests
actors decide. And precisely because of this, knowledge is
always primarily linked, in its generation and initial evaluation, to an interest in prediction and control. Natural science,
history, sociology, are (or potentially are) bodies of knowledge
which serve as resources to facilitate prediction and control in
different contexts. They do not differ in their essential relationship to KCIs. They all arise out of an active instrumental
interest; they may all serve diverse particular interests; they
may all be made the basis of interaction and unconstrained consensus.

With all of this, however, Habermas would disagree; he would
characterise it as rampant scientism, an illegitimate and dangerous
extension of an instrumental conception of knowledge, a misconceived
analysis of interaction as based upon morally indifferent knowledge and arbitrary, irrational evaluation. Unfortunately, we
are provided with no arguments to justify such disagreement, and
no positive alternative account. Habermas does not show how
knowledge can legitimately develop in a context of evaluation
which is not primarily shaped by predictive, instrumental interests. Basically he just doesn't *like* the idea that history and
the human sciences are bodies of instrumentally oriented knowledge, or that, in interactions between people, attempts to predict
and modify the actions of the other occur literally from second
to second. Habermas cannot accept the application of instrumental knowledge to people as normal and appropriate in interaction: to him it is equivalent to treating people as objects;
it is a form of reification. The difference between people and
things should be evident in the forms of knowledge that apply to
them; Habermas does not consider that it may reside instead in
the different procedures and forms of activity which we deploy
in orienting ourselves to people. A properly morally aware orientation to another person is, for Habermas, manifest not just in
attitudes or behaviour, but in the intrinsic character of the
knowledge which it involves. The truth of knowledge should be
explicitly assessed in terms of its relationship to 'the intention
of a good life'. Knowledge is more than a resource for consciousness; it is a strong determinant of consciousness. But this is
asserted and not shown.

Habermas's insistence upon linking science and history to

distinct general interests is based upon only one substantive
factor: this is his firm conviction that science and history are
intrinsically different as bodies of knowledge. Historical knowledge, and 'hermeneutic' knowledge generally, arises from treating thought and activity as *meaningful,* as intelligible only in
terms of some hypothesised general coherent system of meaning.
Hence the 'facts' it deals with are in a sense the products of its
own hypotheses, and do not offer a fully independent check upon
them in the way that facts about real objects could do: acts of
legislation, rights of inheritance, religious observances and the
like are not available as independent existences which can serve
to test historical accounts of legal systems or religions, since
their perceived nature, or even that they are perceived, is a
consequence of the accounts themselves. It follows that the
theoretical speculations of 'hermeneutic' sciences are capable
of evaluation only to the extent that they produce a consistent,
coherent and plausible overall interpretation of activity as
meaningful and intentional. Moreover, since history seeks to
make the past intelligible as the meaningful product of men's thought
and activity, it must reflect all the inconsistency, fluidity of
meaning and adjustment to context characteristic of that thought
and activity itself. Men communicate in ordinary language, which
permits the perpetual renegotiation of meaning, and its adjustment to context in the course of dialogue. Hence the language
of 'hermeneutic' science must also be imprecise and its meaning
context-dependent.

If we accept this description of history and 'hermeneutic'
knowledge (as, in its essentials, we should do), it is clear that
any consensus it achieves cannot be explained in terms of rational
appraisal of an independent reality. This raises the fascinating
and difficult question of how such a consensus is achieved, if
indeed it is ever genuinely 'unconstrained' and more than a consequence of the application of power. For Habermas, consensus in
the hermeneutic sciences is achieved like consensus in the everyday world: people enter into dialogue with a view to the achievement of consensus and evaluate the knowledge they produce with a
view to its relevance to that achievement. Thus, it is part of
the character of hermeneutic knowledge that it is capable of
sustaining a moral community:

[In hermeneutic inquiry] the understanding of meaning is
directed in its very structure toward the attainment of possible
consensus among actors in the framework of a self-understanding
derived from tradition. (p. 310)

Natural science, and instrumental knowledge generally, is taken
by Habermas to be diametrically opposed in its characteristics to
everything set out above. Its referents are held to be fully
independent of its theories and capable of providing separate,
external tests of their instrumental validity; its concepts and
formulations are thought to attain exact definitions and stable
meanings altogether independent of context; its status as 'pure
instrumentality' is held to preclude its operation as a basis for
communal consensus, and it is conceived instead as embedded within
the practice of a scientific community which is sustained by ordinary language interaction involving hermeneutic knowledge (cf.
pp. 138-9).

It is clear that Habermas bases these views on his study of
'positivist' philosophies of science, and is not at all familiar
with its concrete practice. Thus, for all that he provides an
interesting alternative conception of science to that of the
'positivism' he so detests, Habermas's thought, like Lukács's, remains profoundly influenced and misdirected by that very 'positivism'. Openness to fully independent testing, independence of
context, objectively demonstrable rather than communally assigned
validity, are all features which have been imputed to scientific
knowledge by orthodox 'positivist' philosophers of science anxious
to maximise its credibility. Given that all these imputations
are incorrect, it is ironical that Habermas should accept them,
as it were, out of the mouths of his enemies. More ironically
still, orthodox 'positivist' philosophy and history of science
has, in the meantime, itself become aware of the inadequacies
of its earlier formulations and, profiting from its detailed particular studies of science, has been able to show the essential
similarity of scientific and 'hermeneutic' knowledge.

There is no need here to illustrate the context-dependent,
inherently fluid and imprecise character of scientific discourse,
the lack of a clear fact-theory distinction within it, and the
extent to which its status is communally sustained. These points
have been well documented by Mary Hesse (1972) in an excellent
review of Habermas's work, and they are firmly substantiated by
extensive historical study and concretely based argument. (19)
That they are justified is in no way incongruent with the instrumental character of scientific knowledge. All knowledge is made
by men from existing cultural resources; old knowledge is part of
the raw material involved in the manufacture of new; hence,
whatever the interests which guide knowledge generation, socially
sustained consensus and a modification of existing meanings will
always be involved in the process. Habermas, like Lukács, ignores
this essential connection of scientific knowledge with its cultural antecedents, and this constitutes the crucial formal
inadequacy in his account, the central misconception to which all
else can be related. This is why Habermas does not realise that
in describing 'hermeneutic' knowledge, he is merely pointing out
certain universal features of all knowledge. (20)

Let us return now to our earlier hypothesis, that all knowledge
is primarily instrumental. Clearly, nothing said by Habermas
counts against the merits of this view. He does not show knowledge being evaluated without primary regard for predictive or
instrumental standards. He establishes no effective distinction
between instrumental knowledge and other kinds. He offers no
specific criticisms of, for example, an instrumental account of
historical knowledge. He does intend to demonstrate some of
these things when he describes 'hermeneutic' knowledge and the
way it is socially sustained. But what has really to be re-
membered here is that *all* knowledge is socially sustained, a set
of agreed conventions, *as well as* being instrumental in character.
In what follows, it will be assumed that knowledge generally is
primarily instrumental, in the sense that it is generated and
evaluated in a way that is pre-organised by an interest in prediction and control, *and* normative, in the sense that it is

sustained by a communal consensus which is *decided*, and not a rational necessity. (21)

This is not to imply that there are no problems with such an interpretation. On the contrary, the problems are many, and too involved to be dealt with here, where we must simply take what seems the most plausible position and proceed. Perhaps the most difficult problem is how to deal with evaluatively oriented knowledge, on an instrumental view. Everyday discourse is commonly both explicitly evaluative and descriptive. The news media tell us of murders, terrorist attacks, miscarriages of justice and so on. If the above account is to be sustained, we must imagine that the knowledge we acquire from such discourse is to some extent the product of decoding. Terms like 'murder' have a place in networks of concepts theoretically organised to predict and infer what is physically the case. But they also convey information about evaluative orientations. Everyday discourse using such terms can be treated as conveying two kinds of information, rather as an electrical signal can carry both sound and picture information for a television receiver. In both cases, the superimposition of two kinds of information can be achieved with scarcely any interference between the two. We might suggest that everyday discourse *typically* carries two messages in one signal in this way, although whether crossover distortion is typically negligible is another matter. (22)

Such a treatment of the moral component in knowledge is highly contentious. Many serious objections can be brought against it; several philosophical accounts of the essence of moral discourse are difficult to reconcile with it. But alternative empirically oriented accounts are hard to find, as are concretely conceived alternatives to the general instrumental perspective presented here. Habermas would probably condemn the whole account for its insistent separation of the descriptive and the evaluative. But people themselves surely always make some sort of separation of the real and the ideal, that with which they are confronted, and that which they would wish to bring about. Hence, to suggest that they can and do decode discourse to obtain information about actualities and information about ideals is as plausible, in concrete, empirical terms as the rest of the general, instrumental view. Such a view surely deserves consideration as as promising an account of the character of knowledge as any we possess. Certainly, it should not be set aside on the basis of abstract principles which are themselves even more in need of justification.

3 CULTURE AND HISTORY

All knowledge is actively produced by men with particular technical interests in particular contexts; its significance and its scope can never be generalised to the extent that no account is taken of those contexts and interests. Mannheim made this point in the abstract, but never successfully incorporated it into his concrete work. Lukács and Habermas also stressed it, but solely as a basis for large-scale speculation; they both overlooked the character of scientific knowledge as the product of a historical development. Ivins and Gombrich are the only authors so far cited whose understanding of cultural change provides a sufficient basis for a general conception of knowledge. Only they appreciated the way that representations are always built out of pre-existing cultural resources, and hence have always to be explained as developments within an ongoing cultural tradition. (23)   Only they gave detailed examples of how cultural forms actually have developed and changed over time. (24)

It is tempting to suggest that concrete, specific investigation is essential to an adequate general understanding of the character of knowledge and the way that it grows and changes. Familiarity with specific instances would seem a necessary, although certainly not a sufficient, condition of such an understanding. But there is probably a further reason why Gombrich, in writing a detailed commentary on particular pictorial representations, produced a work of greater general theoretical insight than Habermas's cosmological speculations. Gombrich's essay had no need to address the problem of validity; the paintings and other representations he considered were not for the most part thought of as knowledge at all. Habermas, on the other hand, wrote as an epistemologist: validity was his central problem; to pronounce upon the merit and the scope of possible forms of knowledge was his explicit intention.

If genuine knowledge is uniquely determined by the actual, presently existing relationship between the knower and the known, the subject(s) and the objects(s) of knowledge, such problems can be approached with confidence. Only one corpus of genuine knowledge can emerge from the rational perception of reality (as 'positivists' would have it), or the rational investigation of reality in terms predetermined by interests. Such a corpus can be used as a criterion in detecting and criticising error and ideology, and as an end-point for an hypothesised progressive movement in the growth of knowledge. The characteristic epistemological activity of passing judgment upon the knowledge claims of others is thus automatically justified. The most that men can actually hope to achieve in the way of knowledge is conceivable as a final, finished corpus. But if knowledge must *also* be the product of given cultural resources, if rational men must generate knowledge on the basis of what is already thought and believed, then the evaluation of knowledge becomes altogether more problematic.

If old knowledge is indeed a material cause in the generation of new, then man's rationality alone no longer suffices to guarantee him access to a single permanent corpus of genuine knowledge; what he can achieve will depend upon what cognitive resources are available to him, and in what ways he is capable of exploiting such resources. To begin to understand the latter involves abandoning simplistic theories of learning, and undertaking a detailed examination of knowledge generation. To discover the former involves examining knowledge generation in its social context, as part of the history of a particular society and its culture; rational men in different cultures may represent reality in different, even contradictory ways. Hence, the evaluation of knowledge claims is shot through with difficulties; in particular the existing knowledge on the basis of which new knowledge is generated, the culturally given component, can never be independently checked; its origins and justifications in the past are largely inaccessible, nor is there an Archimedean point without the domain of culture, from which to make an assessment of it. To many, this raises the daunting spectre of relativism; for they rightly perceive that standards formulated to judge knowledge must by themselves manufactured from existing resources and historically contingent, if the above account is correct. Small wonder that epistemological writings rarely get directly to grips with these themes. (25)

The problem of relativism should not be of direct concern to a sociological study, and the issues involved cannot in any case be properly considered in the present context. It should suffice us simply to adopt the instrumental ideal of knowledge we have arrived at, and proceed. However, there is a good deal of sociological interest in the problem of relativism, and its discussion does raise some points of naturalistic interest, so a very brief digression on the issue is in order.

For those who wish to avoid relativism, the trouble with the above account is that it offers no naturalistic basis for the objective evaluation of competing knowledge claims, and for the view that knowledge is progressive. Let us then consider whether its essentials can be retained, but its relativistic implications eliminated. Two attempts to do this will be examined; both prove to be unsatisfactory but it is interesting to see why this is so. (26) The first attempt involves postulating that the rational processes by which men learn suffice to produce a convergence in the knowledge of different cultures. Although men have to use their existing knowledge and concepts to make the world intelligible and hence to learn about it, in learning they modify their knowledge in the direction of an ideal final form. They have indeed to start somewhere, but that starting point does not affect where they will eventually end up. A sculptor has to start with a given block of marble when he makes a figure, and the initial shape of the block may continue to influence his work as he proceeds, but we credit him with the ability eventually to realise his figure, whatever initial block he chooses.

This interesting possibility has been very thoroughly investigated by philosophers of science in the inductivist tradition, who would have welcomed its confirmation. So far, their work has produced no grounds for assuming a tendency to such convergence, and the general indication is that no such grounds can be expected to emerge. We must take it, as a provisional, revisable answer to this empirical question, that the cognitive processes which routinely are involved in learning do not suffice to shake off the effect of the given, culturally variable, starting point from which they proceed (cf. Hesse, 1974).

A second possibility is to concentrate upon the cultural resources out of which new knowledge is produced, and question whether these given resources are *merely* conventionally meaningful and consensually sustained. New knowledge, it is agreed, is actively produced from existing knowledge, without necessarily any regard for appearances, or the random flow of phenomena as they are experienced generally. But this is because men are seeking to capture the constantly operating underlying agencies which generate appearances, the real continuing mechanisms at work in the world. To do this they imagine, or create out of existing knowledge, theories about the world - putative mechanisms and agencies, held to exist, and to explain why things are as they are. And then they actively intervene in the course of events to check their theories. Since many mechanisms and forces are thought to exist, they prevent the operation of some, and calculate the effect of others, so that the effect of the mechanism they wish to check becomes apparent. Given that this is what men do, and find profitable, the world must surely be made up of continuing mechanisms and agencies as men imagine. And given that existing knowledge, which postulates particular agencies, is predictively successful, these agencies must surely bear some resemblance to those which really exist.

When scientists attempt to further our understanding of the human body they exploit existing accounts of muscular and skeletal organisation, theories of organic function, and so on. When they investigate chemical compounds and their structures they utilise taken-for-granted knowledge of stable electronic configurations and orbitals. When members analyse their own society they deploy given notions like the 'power' of unions or political groupings, or the 'interests' of classes or occupational groups. In all these cases, knowledge may be developed and extended from a taken-for-granted base. But the base is not arbitrary and *merely* conventional; to have gained acceptance as existing knowledge, it must have come close to describing real existing mechanisms and powers underlying appearances, and presumably it must therefore be capable of describing them more closely still if it is further articulated in the course of active investigation. This gives us a kind of modified correspondence theory of truth: knowledge is not made up of facts which correspond with appearances; it is always a set of given theories, which are evaluated to the extent that they correspond with the powers and mechanisms constantly operative in the world and thus basically constitutive of reality. Our concepts are thus putative real universals which may eventually be modified and developed until they are indeed real universals. They are not just any set of signs and conventions.

There is much to be said for such a position. It is correct to say that the very structure of the knowledge which men produce presumes that reality is constituted in terms of enduring agencies and mechanisms; this is how knowledge gains its essential coherence, and why its verbal component is viably a finite system of symbols. It is also correct to insist that existing knowledge, the material cause of new knowledge, will always embody already the results of learning, and to this extent be more than arbitrary. But neither of these points suffices to discriminate and evaluate different conflicting bodies of knowledge.

Clearly, any group of men believing in some set of real universals can take these universals as the best available rendition of reality, and use them to evaluate different beliefs. We can and do evaluate in this way, but so do those in other cultures, and so did our intellectual ancestors. If we are to regard our

evaluations as special, we must be able to show that our favoured
real explanatory mechanisms and agencies are inherently superior
to or better grounded than anybody elses, that they really are
closest to the real state of things. It is the evident lack of
any way of doing this which deprives our own beliefs about the
basic character of reality of any value as justified independent
standards for the evaluation of knowledge claims generally. (27)

Men in different cultures and societies have understood reality
in a wide variety of ways, invoking diverse causative agencies and
powers allegedly at work in the universe. In simple, tribal,
societies, quasi human agencies - spirits or personified forces -
have often been invoked to explain natural events and human
fortunes. But despite assiduous investigation on the part of
social anthropologists, we have no firm evidence that such beliefs
are inherently unstable, nor is it clear that men who rationally
endeavour to predict and control reality within such anthropo-
morphic cultures must eventually transcend their received perspective and recognise that their scheme of things is erroneous. (28)

It might be thought, nonetheless, that the anthropological
record is not sufficiently powerful evidence in this context.
Tribal beliefs are sometimes alleged not to be related to attempts
to predict and control reality at all, but to be primarily related to other interests (Douglas, 1966). Hence, it is appropriate
to reinforce the argument by reference to the culture of the
natural sciences, the primarily instrumental interests of which
can scarcely be doubted.

It is well known that as scientific knowledge has developed
numerous mechanisms and theories have been postulated and succes-
sively set aside. This is, indeed, why so many philosophers of
science have struggled to maintain a fact/theory distinction, and
to base their justificatory rhetoric on the accumulation of facts.
But there has also been a good deal of informal faith placed in
the progressive quality of this sequence of theories and mechanisms. Recent historical studies, however, in particular those of
T. S. Kuhn (1970), effectively undermine this faith; they demonstrate that fundamental theoretical transitions in science are not
simply rational responses to increased knowledge of reality,
predictable in terms of context-independent standards of inference
and evaluation. Such transitions make very good sense as responses to perceived practical problems, or as correlates of
technical and procedural reorganisation within particular scientific communities. They are intelligible enough when referred to
actual situations where new findings or new instrumentations are
emerging. To this extent, they certainly are not manifestations
of scientific irrationality, or mysterious emotional reorienta-
tions. But they do not possess the kind of general features
which would be required by the progressive realism we are considering: it cannot be said that there is less of reality left
to explain after such a transition, or that any part of the
world is finally explained, or even necessarily that scientists
perceive themselves as having fewer problems afterwards. Nor
are we ever in a position to say that scientists could not
properly have done other than they did. We simply do not find,
when actual instances are studied, that the case for a particular

theoretical change can be established in context-independent terms.
It is never unambiguously clear that existing theories could not
have reasonably been maintained, or that yet other theories might
not have been produced with just as much to recommend them.

Progressive realism is one of the ideal accounts of scientific
knowledge which has it moving toward something, in this case a
description of the real existing mechanisms in the world. There
are now several independent strands of work which imply that such
theories are misconceived, and that all knowledge generation and
cultural growth should be regarded as endlessly dynamic and suscep-
tible to alteration just as is human activity itself, with every
actual change or advance a matter of agreement and not necessity.
Even the long-standing Popperian tradition provides an adequate
feel for these points; it provides many examples of the dialectical
character of science, and the way it feeds upon an ever expanding
number of self-generated problems, producing more work for itself
with every accomplishment (rather than less, through disposing of
'part of reality'). Imre Lakatos's brilliant study of the history
of Euler's Theorem (1963) is an outstanding illustration of how
much there is to be learned from this tradition. But two recent
general approaches to semantic change, which cannot be discussed
here, convey even more clearly the merits of such a view. One
is the interaction view of metaphor, and the fully general account
of meaning and meaning change it involves. The other is the
ethnomethodological treatment of the indexical and reflexive
properties of verbal utterances. Although apparently distinct
independent academic traditions are involved, there are interesting parallels between them, which derive from their common reliance
on the late work of Ludwig Wittgenstein. (29)

The upshot of all this is that our current scientific models
and mechanisms are likely to be seen at some future time as part
of what is an endlessly unfolding chain of such mechanisms, constructed and eventually abandoned (or stripped of their ontological
standing) as the activity of knowledge generation proceeds.
Clearly then our present theories should stand symmetrically with
earlier scientific theories, and for that matter with any other
instrumentally oriented knowledge, in all sociologically relevant
respects. The diverse real universals postulated at different
times and in different cultures and contexts, should be regarded
alike as inventions of the mind, sustained to the extent that
they are instrumentally valuable in the settings where they are
found. There is no means of going further and ranking or evaluating them in a way which does not simply *assume* the priority of one
or other of them.

Knowledge cannot be understood as more than the product of men
operating in terms of an interest in prediction and control
shaped and particularised by the specifics of their situations. It
is not the unique possession of any particular culture or type
of culture. Wherever men deploy their cultural resources to
authentic tasks of explanation and investigation indicated by their
interests, what they produce deserves the name of knowledge. (30)
It deserves sociological study (and naturalistic or scientific
study generally) as a typical example of knowledge. There is no
more strictly defined conception which would discriminate say

between 'scientific' knowledge, and other kinds, and justify
different forms of sociological investigation in the two cases.
We can study the process of knowledge generation, and fill out
our general understanding of how it unfolds, by observing *any*
culture wherein change is occurring under the impetus of an interest
in prediction and control. (31)

What then of the problem of relativism? The first thing to be
said of this is that whatever conclusions are reached on the matter
should not count against the preceding discussion. If one is
interested in exploring and extending the possibilities of naturalistic thought and investigation, one does not turn back because
its consequences prove unpleasant. If we cannot find any naturalistic basis for differentially evaluating the knowledge of
different cultures, then that is that. If epistemologists and
ontologists face problems as a consequence, they must simply be
accepted. What matters is that we recognise the *sociological*
equivalence of different knowledge claims. We will doubtless continue to evaluate beliefs differentially ourselves, but such
evaluations must be recognised as having no relevance to the task
of sociological explanation; as a methodological principle we
must not allow our evaluation of beliefs to determine what form
of sociological account we put forward to explain them.

It is sometimes felt that such arguments must be rejected simply
because they represent a concession to relativism. Relativism is
often opposed in sociology as a matter of passion and commitment,
even by those who recognise the lack of any good arguments for
their case. It is felt that to do otherwise is to provide a
licence for any kind of nonsensical thought, and to display a
lack of interest in what the world is really like.

Although there is no need to offer concessions to such an unsatisfactory position, it should be emphasised that the merits of
relativism as a philosophical position are not argued for here.
Nobody is enjoined to value all knowledge equally, or to choose
which they will employ with a coin or a die. The prejudice of the
argument is rather thoroughly naturalistic; it is naturalism which
is being employed and advocated. The naturalistic equivalence of
the knowledge of different cultures is merely a finding, something
which happens to be the case. To be sure, it implies the conventional status of naturalism itself, but this is no disaster.
It does not imply the abandonment of naturalism in favour of a
frantic search for necessity elsewhere. One can choose to continue
with the relevant activities.

Naturalism, moreover, implies the most intensely serious
concern with what is real, and a particular, concretely relevant
conception of it is actually advocated here. Everything of
naturalistic significance would indicate that there is indeed one
world, one reality, 'out there', the source of our perceptions if
not their total determinant, the cause of our expectations being
fulfilled or disappointed, of our endeavours succeeding or being
frustrated. But this reality should not be identified with any
linguistic account of it, or, needless to say, with any way of
perceiving it, or pictorial representation of it. Reality is the
source of *primitive causes,* which, having been pre-processed by
our perceptual apparatus, produce changes in our knowledge and

the verbal representations of it which we possess. All cultures
relate symmetrically to this reality. Men in all cultures are
capable of making reasonable responses to the causal inputs they
receive from reality - that is, are capable of learning. (32)
That the structure of our verbal knowledge does not thereby
necessarily converge upon a single form, isomorphous with what
is real, should not surprise us. Why ever should we expect this
to be a property of our linguistic and cognitive capabilities?

Chapter 2

THE PROBLEM OF IDEOLOGY

1 THE CONCEPT OF IDEOLOGY

Current usage of the terms 'ideology' and 'ideological determination' is hopelessly loose and variable. This is the case even
when they are applied only to putative descriptions of reality
and not to moral positions, ideals, political programmes etc.
At one extreme are usages which effectively devalue all beliefs
and concepts alike; at the other, only the products of cynically
propagandist, manipulative intentions are impugned. This blurring
of meaning is unfortunate, for, although conceptions of ideology
and ideological determination have never been sufficiently clearly
focused, in their most characteristic sociological usages they do
possess particular implications which are worth keeping distinct.
They treat of beliefs and aspects of culture in a way which is
both pejorative and genuinely explanatory in a naturalistic sense.
Beliefs are held to be ideologically determined if they are
created, accepted or sustained, in the particular form that they
have, only because they are related to particular social interests.
Such interests are among the causes of the beliefs, or of the form
in which they are found; they help to explain why the beliefs
have the form that they do have. And since this is so, the beliefs
are held to be exposed as inadequate or as inadequately grounded.

To what extent can the essentials of this usage be retained, in
the light of the conception of knowledge offered in the previous
chapter? Can we still define ideologies by their relationship to
particular social interests? And can we still impute inadequacy to
such beliefs, given that we have renounced appeals to how reality
actually is, or to ideals of disinterested contemplation, as bases
for evaluation?

To attempt to answer these questions it is useful to turn to
Marx, and his extensive critical discussions of bourgeois economic
thought. (1) There are a number of different conceptions of
ideology run together in these discussions. Occasionally, Marx
used his own theory of capitalism as a test for other beliefs:
those which contradicted it were revealed as ideologies obscuring
and concealing reality. Occasionally too, he treated ideology as
little different from propaganda; this was particularly the case

when he dealt with 'vulgar bourgeois thought', and the more
blatant polemicists of political economy. But the dominant account
of ideology in Marx's work is altogether more satisfactory and
interesting. It is particularly evident in his criticisms of the
political economy of Smith and Ricardo, in 'Capital', in 'Theories
of Surplus Value' (1969), and elsewhere.

Marx was in no way dismissive of the work of the serious political economists. These were men concerned to understand an
emerging set of social forms, in order to sustain them and make
them work. Their theorising had to be practical and predictive
if it was to serve its intended purposes; they needed, we might
loosely say, to stay in touch with reality. (2) And so successfully did the best of them do this that Marx, the most insightful
of their critics, readily acknowledged his debt to their ideas and
modes of analysis.

What was mainly at fault with the work of such thinkers as
Smith and Ricardo, so far as Marx was concerned, was the restricted
scope of their analyses, which derived in turn from the particular
interests in terms of which they operated. As later writers put
it, these interests acted as a filter upon experience; they
intensified the investigation of some aspects of social and economic relationships and led to others being ignored.

Thus, political economy addressed itself to an hypothetical
matrix of social interactions, all of which had the character of
commodity exchanges between individuals engaged in satisfying their
own interests to the maximum possible extent. By considering
such a matrix as an isolated system, the political economists
assessed its overall responses to such factors as general changes
in supply and demand, and hence they claimed to be in a position
to predict actual economic trends in particular societies. The
economies of societies were treated as isolated sets of relationships which really corresponded to the hypothetical form, yet it
was a particular concern with this form of relationship, and not
detailed empirical study of the economic interactions in particular
societies, which had led to its initial consideration.

Moreover, analysis of the behaviour of the matrix (the market)
was conditioned by interest. Analysis was effectively designed
to answer a limited range of technical questions, all concerned
with the normal, stable operation of this ideal economic system;
the bourgeois theorists sought to secure and stabilise it, not to
overthrow it. Hence, their discussion of rent and profit concentrated on the properties which rent and profit possessed as
variables within their ideal system. There was little interest
in the historical processes which generate rights to rent or
profit, or the distribution of power which makes rents or profits
enforceable rights. Nor was there any concern with the conditions
under which these rights, or the very activity of commodity ex-
change itself, might cease to operate. Indeed, even when consideration of the market suggested, as it did to Ricardo, that
its *normal operation* itself generated dynamic, destabilising forces
over the long term, there was no noticeable shift of attention
toward the problem. The high point of the emergence of competitive capitalism was not the place to meditate on the determinants
of its decline. The conditions of its stable operation were of

greater relevance, and demonstrations of self-regulatory mechanisms
in that operation were particularly welcome. The only significant
move by the political economists from a synchronic to a long-term,
diachronic, historical perspective is exemplified by the work of
Malthus, which was an attempt to demonstrate the essential *stability*
of the level of wages.

This concern with those features of the market which maintained
it as a stable system helps to explain how the political economists
treated their central terms. They had no cause to subject such
terms as 'rent', 'profit' or 'wage' to more than a minimum of
elucidation. It was the co-variation of the magnitude of these
terms, generated by their interconnection in a given system, which
was the focus of attention; they could be treated almost as the
'x's and 'y's in an algebraic equation.

With this kind of analysis, Marx revealed the limited scope of
political economy without being forced to appeal to some objective
reality. He noted the neglect of problems recognised to some
extent as problems by Smith and Ricardo themselves, and restrictions
in their thinking which they themselves would have, and in some
cases had, acknowledged. The value of his critical commentary is
immense. But we must examine, none the less, the precise force
and character of Marx's criticism, and how far it reflects upon
the adequacy of the knowledge in question.

It might be claimed that Marx revealed the inadequacy and in-
authenticity of political economy as an attempt at prediction and
control. How could an ideal-type like 'the market' have been
taken seriously as an aid to the prediction of economic phenomena
in concrete societies? (3) How, in the absence of *full* knowledge
of the factors which sustained or undermined the market system,
could one assume its continuing existence in any society, as a
basis for economic prediction? Had not expedient interests, by
narrowing the range of bourgeois thought, effectively made it
instrumentally inapplicable?

This is indeed a worthwhile line to follow, but we should not
overestimate its possibilities. Let us compare the political
economists' knowledge of 'the market' with anatomists' knowledge
of 'the arm' as presented, say, in Figure 1.3 (p. 9). Here is
another abstraction, which, as we have noted already, does not
convey information about any particular arm. Nor does it indicate
anything about the arm's systemic stability; it ignores the possibility of muscular movement, tissue degeneracy, growth, ageing and
death; it marks neither lesions, tumours, blood-clots nor
fractures.

Anatomical knowledge is focused around a particular narrow perspective, the product of the development of science and medicine.
It is sustained and restricted by a structure of particular
technical interests reflecting the professional divisions between
different specialisms. Nor are these interests merely restrictions on the range of anatomists' investigations. If medical
science has advanced along a broader, less specialised front,
there is no reason to suppose that, as a sub-set of its knowledge,
there would have been produced the same terms, classifications,
representations or even theories as those found within the
province of anatomy today. Interest does not affect a body of

knowledge by determining what sub-group of truths will be included within it; interest pervasively influences the overall knowledge generating activity. As products of particular technical interests, 'the market' and 'the arm' stand symmetrically.

Yet, anatomical knowledge manifestly is applicable, and is applied in particular cases. Nor are those who employ it embarrassed by its lack of a diachronic dimension, or an etiology, or by its failure to predict or describe particular cases. This knowledge is a *resource* generated in conjunction with a form of activity, to aid the activity; and practitioners learn in what context, and how, the resource is utilisable. They can decide when to use the knowledge alone; when to combine it with physiology, pathology or biophysics; when to shrug their shoulders and try something else; even when to suggest a modification of the knowledge itself. Yet the way in which these decisions are routinely accomplished may be different to verbalise, or even unverbalis-able. Nor can the anatomist ever convincingly show (nor presumably does he believe) that having invoked so much additional knowledge, scientific or common sense, to assist in a problem, he has at any point a 'full' or 'total' comprehension of it.

Analogously, a model market mechanism could serve as a resource in the solution of particular problems, such as what happens to wages as fixed capital accumulates in a given context. And further cultural resources could be brought in as thought necessary to particular situations: Ricardo, for example, made considerable use of the 'psychological' generalisation that owners of capital preferred to place it close at hand and under personal super-vision, when he considered the effects of different patterns of international trade. There is no reason why knowledge of 'the market' should be considered less applicable than knowledge of 'the arm'. (One might consider that the latter arose from a more intimate and thorough acquaintance with its purported subject than did the former, and would thus be less likely to include what practitioners would straightforwardly acknowledge as error; but that is another matter.)

Like political economy, anatomy exists, in the precise form that we know it, as a response to particular interests in predic-tion and control, which are in turn related to social interests. All knowledge claims emerge out of activities and evaluations pre-structured by such interests. It is of the nature of knowledge that it develops in terms of particular interests and, as seen from other perspectives, ignores aspects or characteristics of the phenomena or situations it studies. Thus, in so far as Marx criti-cised political economy *solely* for its restricted scope he did not differentiate it from other knowledge.

His analysis remains of very great value. And, at the time, the scope of political economy needed delineation to a degree which is rarely paralleled in natural scientific fields. Practice tells scientists in what way to rely upon their knowledge; they appreci-ate its standing and scope because they operate in the context wherein it arose, and where its use is simultaneously an applica-tion and an ongoing test of it. And this appreciation, without being either complete or immune to criticism, is essential to their deployment of their knowledge as a resource. (4) Yet there is

little need to verbalise and formalise it because of the way in
which scientific organisation tends to restrict its use to 'in-
siders'. In contrast, political economy was presented to a wide
range of audiences, many of which had interests and perspectives
divergent from those of its originators, and different backgrounds of social experience.

It might be said that the important distinction between anatomy
and political economy is the role of *class* interests, which are
significant only in relation to the latter set of knowledge claims;
None the less, this precise form of analysis should not be taken
as indicating the ideological character of political economy. The
grounds for saying this are merely those of terminological con-
venience, but they remain important. The terms 'ideology' and
'ideological determination' have generally been used to *discriminate* knowledge claims, to cut them into two kinds. And, as
we shall see, there is a way in which they can continue to do this
with as much sociological import as ever. If such a usage is
abandoned in favour of one where all knowledge is 'ideological', the
terms lose much of their capacity for doing sociological work. They
merely serve to remind us of the contingency of all knowledge and
the way it is always related to particular interests, and this
is automatically done for us by the conception of knowledge we have
already developed.

It might be said that the important distinction between anatomy
and political economy is the role of *class* interests, which are
significant only in relation to the latter set of knowledge claims;
it is these interests which give political economy its character
as an ideology. Certainly, such a strategy of definition produces
a cut between ideologically determined beliefs and other kinds,
but it is hard to see the value of the cut when one's aim, as here,
is to understand the general relationship of interests and beliefs,
and not yet to link them to social-structural factors. (5)

Accordingly, another strategy of definition is adopted here,
again inspired by Marx's work and appropriately illustrated by
reference to his criticism of the political economists. In the
end, we shall agree with Marx that even the best political economy
was ideologically determined. And we shall have as well a definition of ideological determination with both naturalistic significance and some degree of pejorative implication.

In 'Theories of Surplus Value', Marx provided a detailed, concrete
examination of the 'contradictions' in the thinking of Smith and
Ricardo. One of the most basic in a series of related contradictions in Smith's thought is an inconsistency in the definition
of value. Sometimes Smith held the value of a commodity to be
given by the amount of labour time involved in producing it, or, as
Marx sometimes said, by the amount of labour materially incorporated
into it. Sometimes value was held to be the amount of living
labour which the commodity would buy. In a penetrating discussion,
this inconsistency is shown to be the cause of a whole series of
problems in Smith's theories, many of which were recognised by
Smith himself, who even, at times, revealed himself to be aware
of the contradiction at the root of them. Its consequences are
traced into discussions of commodity prices, levels of profit and
rent, and many other fields. And its subsequent influence upon
other writers, notably Ricardo, is documented in detail.

Marx's own view of this aberration, which he himself set to
rights with his well-known theory of value, was that it stemmed

from the limited perspective of Smith's thinking, consequent upon his identification with bourgeois interests. Being a bourgeois, to whom profit was 'natural', and values and prices as found in the competitive marketplace the centre of attention, the crucial data relevant to the resolution of the contradiction were far from the centre of his vision (cf. 1969, vol. 2, pp. 216-22).

Such criticism is too gentle. Marx himself revealed the definition of value to have been of major importance to Smith and the relevant data to have occupied a significant place in his consciousness. Surely Marx's own commentary suggests that Smith was inconsistent because to admit that living labour could be bought for far less than the value of what it produced undermined his *rationalisation* of the market economy. Although a serious and realistic thinker, Smith was actively concerned to *justify* an idealised 'bourgeois' order, and to show that its existence was in the interest of all economic classes. Where his own instrumentally oriented speculations led him toward contrary conclusions, there was a tendency for him to turn them aside or lay them over with rationalisations - claims invented to serve expedient social interests and *not* directly instrumental ones. It is the role of these rationalisation-generating interests, and not the existence of contradictions, that marks out Smith's work, and political economy generally, as ideologically determined. The evident contradictions which Marx pointed out are merely signs of the clash between direct instrumental interests guiding thought and investigation, and interests of a less reputable kind. (6)

Most of the contradictions Marx revealed in political economy are indeed signs of ideological determination, and not accidents of inference or the consequences of technical restrictions upon investigation. Adam Smith's vagueness about 'natural value' arose because Smith wanted the actual value of commodities to turn out in fact to be a *just* value. Ricardo's unsatisfactory discussion of monopolies and cartels arose because naturalistic investigation led him toward the view that they could be expedient in some circumstances, but political interest demanded that they be exposed as economically inferior to laissez-faire policies. Example after example could be cited. Political economy was through and through ideologically determined, even when it was produced by men with predominantly instrumental, naturalistic orientations. Although neither Smith nor Ricardo sought to manufacture pure rationalisations after the manner of Malthus, and what Marx called 'vulgar political economy', their thought was affected at another level so that their naturalistic conclusions were modulated and amended.

Let us now try to clarify the conception of ideological determination which is involved here. We have already described how men bring their cultural resources and cognitive proclivities to bear to solve authentic, direct problems of prediction and control. But such resources and proclivities can also be deployed with a mind to other problems: 'What account of reality would lead others to act so that instead of furthering their own interests, as they intend, they further ours?' 'In what kind of world would the institutions we support be stable and accepted?', and so on. On few occasions are such problems the sole inspiration of thought and knowledge generation, since the pure

rationalisation which would result from this would, in many contexts, lack credibility. But instrumentally oriented thinking is
often modulated by, or even ruled by such concerns, so that it
generates descriptions other than those it would otherwise have
produced. Such descriptions can serve social interests, in
attempts to deceive others or by consolatory self-deception, only
if they possess the credibility which comes from being falsely
perceived as genuine attempts to solve direct instrumental problems. The provenance of such beliefs must necessarily be concealed
if they are to have any chance of gaining credibility and hence of
functioning. Thus, it is expedient to keep them as close as
possible to the indications of authentic instrumentally oriented
thought, in order that they might pass as the consequences of
such thought. (7)

Hence, wherever knowledge is ideologically determined there is
disguise or concealment of an interest which generates or sustains
the knowledge, or, to put it another way, of the problem to which
the knowledge is actually a solution. This gives us a basis for
the definition of ideological determination. Knowledge or culture
is ideologically determined in so far as it is created, accepted
or sustained by concealed, unacknowledged, illegitimate interests.

If we accept this definition of ideological determination we
have a concept which plays a role in naturalistic explanation, and
which has an obvious pejorative significance given that its
application will, in practice, adversely influence credibility,
and actual judgments of the adequacy of beliefs. It is a wider
ranging term than 'propaganda', since individuals may very well
be unaware of the interests and the cognitive processes involved
when they create or evaluate knowledge. And, finally, it is a
definition which involves no claim that those using it possess
privileged access to reality.

2 PROBLEMS OF APPLICATION

It is important to note some specific implications of the definition of ideological determination offered above, and to consider
some of the considerable technical difficulties involved in its
application. In particular contexts, beliefs may meaningfully be
treated as ideologically determined, or even called 'ideologies',
to the extent that concealed interests are thought to influence
the people who sustain and propagate them. But one must guard
against regarding such descriptions as references to the intrinsic
properties of beliefs or representations. Beliefs are not ideological in the way that billiard balls are red.

A belief or set of beliefs does not carry the distorted imprint
of reality, as it were, as a physical feature, if it is ideologically determined. One cannot detect a tangible effect of
ideological determination either by examining a belief itself or
by comparing it with the reality it allegedly describes. Nor,
moving from a realist to an instrumentalist perspective, does a
belief reflect in its own intrinsic nature whatever ideological
function it was created to perform, so that it becomes useless as
a resource for anything else. There is no particular reason why

beliefs related to concealed interests in one context should not
be sustained in another as resources serving an overt interest in
prediction and technical control. The mode of determination of
beliefs in particular contexts cannot be used as an indication of
their inherent character, and it is probably best to avoid the
danger of doing this by refraining from characterising them as
'ideological', and pedantically treating them as ideologically
determined in specified contexts and situations. (8)

How, though, are we to demonstrate that beliefs are so determined in particular contexts? How are we to demonstrate the
operation of concealed interests? This is an important theoretical question which is also of practical relevance, since the
identification of such interests almost always implies a lowering
of the credibility of knowledge in particular contexts. (9)   In
this section, the question will be considered in a restricted
form, as a problem of understanding individual acts of creation,
acceptance or transmission of knowledge. When the technical problems raised at this level have been considered the discussion
will move to a broader, more typically sociological standpoint.

Since there is nothing in the intrinsic character of a belief
to reveal its provenance or the interests which were operative
in its production, there is a technical difficulty in establishing
an account of that provenance, invoking concealed interests, as
superior to a legitimating account of it, citing legitimate
interests only.   Wherever beliefs are ideologically determined
their supporters represent them otherwise - they legitimate them.
And the legitimation can rarely be refuted by any simple objective
test. We may suspect that Malthusian political economy was an
'ex post facto' rationalisation of certain policies and evaluations: it was presented as the product of an effort to understand
and predict social processes as they did and would occur. We may
suspect that some current hereditarian accounts of racial differences are inspired by concealed interests: they are presented as
nothing more than assessments of which theories best account for
currently accepted evidence in certain areas of investigation.
How are we to decide whether or not our suspicions are correct?

Ideally, we would say that Malthus, with his accepted beliefs
and cultural resources, *could* not have arrived at his pessimistic
analysis simply via a rational attempt to understand and predict.
Or that hereditarian hypotheses, in some cases, just do not inspire
the degree of rational conviction their proponents claim, given
the evidence they point to and the cultural background they assume
or rely on. But we lack a theory of natural rationality sufficiently precise and detailed to be taken as the basis for claims
of this kind. We are not in a position to show that the cognitive propensities of actors, in a given cultural context, would
or would not lead them to theorise in a particular way simply out
of a legitimate interest in understanding and prediction.

Moreover, what we do know of cognition only serves to emphasise
the difficulty of identifying concealed interests in many cases.
Often, we suspect their involvement where we find *isomorphisms*
in beliefs (cf. Huaco, 1971), that is, where the structure of one
set of beliefs is mirrored in another (and the one, typically, is
invoked to legitimate the other). Thus, Marx noted how the Holy

Family reflects the structure of the ideal earthly family and is used to legitimate it. 'Bourgeois' individualism found expression in philosophies of nature which in turn served as a resource in legitimating capitalist institutions. Academic accounts of knowledge frequently divide it into inherently distinct categories, so that its structure serves as a justification for the isomorphous structure of academic organisation and social control. In all these cases, it is tempting to cite concealed interests as relevant determinants. Yet we cannot do so simply upon the basis of isomorphism. Theorising of any kind, inspired by any interest, involves the creation and extension of metaphors and analogies. Explanation and understanding, in science as anywhere else, involves conceptualising the unfamiliar in terms of the familiar (Barnes, 1974). Such processes inevitably generate isomorphisms between different sub-systems of meanings within a culture. How far these isomorphisms are the products of instrumental, or of concealed social interests, is a matter demanding further investigation; the mere existence of isomorphism is unrevealing in itself.

There simply is not, at the present time, any explicit, objective set of rules or procedures by which the influence of concealed interests upon thought and belief can be established. However, it remains possible in many instances to identify the operation of concealed interests by a subjective, experimental approach. Where an actor gives a legitimating account of his adhesion to a belief or set of beliefs we can test that account in the laboratory of our own consciousness. Adopting the cultural orientation of the actor, programming ourselves with his programmes, we can assess what plausibility the beliefs possess for us. In so far as our cognitive proclivities can be taken as the same as those of the actor, our assessment is evidence of the authenticity of his account.

This is, of course, merely to rely upon a standard kind of sociological investigation using what Weber referred to as 'erklärendes Verstehen' and is loosely characterised by a wide variety of notions such as 'empathy' and 'taking the role of the other'. The essence of what is involved has been exquisitely formulated by Lévi-Strauss: 'every human mind is a locus of virtual experience where what goes on in the minds of men, however remote they may be, can be investigated' (1962, p. 176).

All too often this mode of investigation is either apologised for or celebrated as the obverse of 'objective' scientific investigation. It is no such thing. It is genuinely empirical and experimental. And it is capable of intersubjective checking and replication as much as any scientific procedure. (10) The difficulties it raises are all technical and methodological, though none the less daunting for that. How to be sure that we have correctly taken into account the orientation of the other actor is a continuing problem. How to resolve matters when different investigators come to different conclusions on the basis of their 'virtual experience' is likewise acutely problematic.

But such technical difficulties should not obscure the fact that the approach can be successfully applied in a considerable number of instances. Where, for example, actors legitimate their suspect beliefs by presenting them as the implications of accepted

knowledge and procedure, the legitimation can be checked by
virtual experience. And reasonable confidence can often be placed
in the result of the check, particularly when the knowledge and
procedure appealed to is highly systematised and strongly bounded.
Let us establish this point firmly in principle by citing a
ludicrously improbable example. Suppose that, in the furtherance
of some concealed interest, it was claimed that $2 + 2 = 5$. And
suppose also that the claim was 'justified' as an implication of
current mathematical knowledge and procedure. In practice, such a
justification would readily be checked and dismissed. There
would probably be no problem in deciding upon the relevant cultural
conventions to take as background, and no controversy between
investigators. The belief, accounted in the legitimation as following from normal mathematical practice, would be revealed as a
departure from that practice by investigation through virtual experience. The task would be simple and consensus generating;
mathematical procedures in this area are remarkably standardised,
and effectively sustained in their standard forms by mathematical
socialisation. (11)

It is a very common form of legitimation to claim that a belief
follows from or is strongly supported by the normal procedures of
some valued institution, in particular, science or one of its
constituent fields. And, given the strongly defined procedures and
clearly marked-off cultural resources of modern scientific dis-
ciplines, it is often practically possible to ascertain where such
beliefs do depart from normal scientific practice and hence where
they may be the products of concealed interests masquerading as
scientific results. (12) Thus, our example, involving detection
of a departure from normal practice in the area of mathematics,
exemplifies an important class of instances. It is an unlikely
example only because, for the only concealed interest it could
plausibly serve, the deception and manipulation of others, it
lacks the potential credibility which would be essential for it
to be put to use. Where people support their (suspect) beliefs
by appeal to science, as in the race/IQ debate, the controversies
over environmental pollution, the current ethological pronouncements on 'human nature', or the polemics against cannabis use,
they are generally careful to ensure that deviation from normal
scientific practice is not apparent at a casual glance. In
general it will be extremely difficult to check in terms of virtual
experience whether or not a suspect knowledge claim does evidently
'follow' from the accepted knowledge to which its legitimation
relates it. (13)

In the previous section, some aspects of Adam Smith's economic
views were held to be ideologically determined. It was suggested
that some of the implications of his general theoretical position
were avoided or set aside, probably for the sake of concealed
interests, and that special pleading and rationalisation replaced
authentic applications of his theories in some contexts. The only
basis for this claim must lie in where Smith's presuppositions take
our own thought when we experimentally adopt them and proceed upon
their basis. Only our virtual experience gives us any grounds
for holding Smith's analysis of value to be a departure from the
normal practice of his economics - that is from the normal practice

by reference to which he rationalised and legitimated the analysis.
And in this case our hypothesis must be much more tentative than
in the preceding imaginary example, and hence more typical of what
can be hoped for in practice. We lack a sufficiently clear picture
of Smith's economic thought, and the common-sense assumptions and
everyday knowledge he would routinely have referred to in developing it. And the thought and the knowledge in question are doubtless themselves unclear, unsystematic, inconsistent. Hence we are
very limited in the extent to which we can surmise how Smith would
have approached the problem of value had his interests been entirely
legitimate. We have only a vague and tentative basis upon which
to infer what were normal procedures of economic analysis and
what problematic departures therefrom. This, and not the less
problematic contexts of mathematics and the systematic sciences, is
typical of situations in which sociological investigations must
proceed.

Clearly, there is great technical difficulty involved in identifying the role of concealed interests when they divert thought and
belief away from standardised routes and patterns, or from what
might generally be characterised as normal practice. Even though
the aim of this section has been to suggest ways of achieving such
identifications, and to advocate their use, these technical problems are not to be denied. Indeed, the discussion must conclude
on an even more pessimistic mote. In those many instances where
concealed interests are not to be exposed by reference to normal
practice, the task of revealing their operation is even more
difficult. How are such interests to be identified when they
inspire major innovations which involve explicit rejection of existing parts of the system of culture? On what basis does one generate
virtual experience which can be taken as that of the innovating
actor, and on what basis does one evaluate it? In particular, if
the innovation is legitimated purely as an hypothesis or likely
speculation, how does one cast doubt upon the legitimation to the
extent of suggesting that in the absence of concealed interests
the speculation would not have been made? It is hard to imagine
that many original speculations upon racial differences, human
aggressiveness, the different inherent nature of the male and
female, the future of capitalism, and so on, have not been inspired
or influenced by various concealed expedient interests. But how
their role in *speculation* is to be assessed, even via recourse to
virtual experience, it is difficult to say. The difficulty of
the task contrasts starkly with the confidence with which sociologists and polemicists typically undertake it.

3 LEVELS OF ANALYSIS

It should not be thought that the preceding analysis of ideological
determination is a restrictive one, which treats it as an effect
lying, as it were, around the edges of knowledge. What has been
said does not trivialise the concept. On the contrary, legitimation, rationalisation, self-consolation are demands which constantly
bear upon the generation and maintenance of all knowledge, and
which cannot be made explicit by actors themselves without lowering

the credibility of the knowledge in question. There is little or
no knowledge which does not to some extent reflect in its content
the operation of unacknowledged interests; there is no knowledge where such interests do not influence its organisation and
distribution. Knowledge grows under the impulse of two great
interests, an overt interest in prediction manipulation and control,
and a covert interest in rationalisation and persuasion. Our
definition of ideological determination has essentially identified
it as the mode of operation of this second great interest.

It might be objected that the policy of symmetrical, naturalistic, non-evaluative investigation has here completely broken down.
Knowledge has just been described as developing under the impetus
of two great interests, yet one of them is built into our basic
conception of knowledge and the other is presented separately,
subordinately and, implicitly at least, as a factor which de-
values the knowledge it has affected. The naturalistic justification for this is that actors themselves operate on the basis of
just such a distinction. Typically, they themselves reject knowledge claims which are perceived as nothing more than legitimations. They themselves treat the two great interests asymmetric-
ally.

Such a justification relies upon an empirical claim. If it
could be shown that actors would accept and utilise knowledge to
the extent that they were convinced of its status as a legitimation, then indeed the asymmetrical treatment above would need
modification. But for the present it seems safe enough. It is
true that many beliefs do persist as legitimations and nothing
more. And it is true also that social anthropologists have analysed
whole systems of belief, and explained their persistence, by
reference to legitimating functions and little else. It remains
the case that in these instances the provenance of the beliefs
is concealed by, or unknown to, the relevant actors, and that such
beliefs are employed indirectly in attempts to influence others
and not directly as immediate guides to action.

In any event, to give a different standing to the two kinds of
interest that bear upon the production of knowledge does not
really affect the symmetrical treatment of knowledge itself. We
are not led to talk of two distinct kinds of knowledge as a consequence, since any knowledge may be sustained by either or both
kinds of interest. Nor must we regard ideologically determined
knowledge as being irrationally sustained. As was shown earlier,
it is best thought of as a naturally rational response to a need
for legitimation, which is then transmitted, sustained or undermined by the same social processes as operate with knowledge of
any kind. Its provenance is concealed - generally it is disguised
as a rational response to an instrumental problem - to facilitate
and enlarge the extent of its sustenance and transmission by
such social processes.

The great and pervasive importance of concealed interests was
obscured in the previous section by its concentration on particular
acts of knowledge generation or transmission. This can now be
set right by considering their operation at the institutional
level, that is, as they cumulatively affect knowledge as an
institution. There are two aspects to this problem. The first

involves consideration of how concealed interests influence knowledge as a linked, ongoing set of shared representations; this will
be discussed here. The second involves relating concealed interests
and the representations they sustain to social structure. This
may be considered as a particular instance of the problem of
interrelating knowledge, interests and social structure generally,
something discussed in the next chapter as the problem of *imputation* in the sociology of knowledge. Moving from the individual
to the institutional level of analysis simplifies some problems
but creates others, as far as relating knowledge and concealed
interests is concerned. Let us use a concrete example to illustrate what is involved. J. S. Haller's (1971) study of the
'scientific' accounts of negro-white differences produced in the
USA in the late nineteenth century will serve very well. Haller
catalogues a long list of explanations of the mental inferiority
of the negro, all of which tended to be pessimistic with regard to
the possibility of ameliorating either his cognitive or his
spiritual inadequacies.

The explanations in question invoked the experimental results
of anthropometry and in particular craniometry, citing measures
of facial angle, and brain size and weight. Later they appealed
to the evolutionary theories of the post-Darwin period, claiming
that many of his physical attributes placed the negro lower than
the white in the evolutionary hierarchy, and correspondingly closer
to animal kinds. And throughout the period they appealed to
behavioural evidence such as the abbreviated period of negro
infancy, and the restricted educability of negroes, based largely
on their capacity for imitation. All of this material was deployed
to justify the view that negro-white differences were real, in-
herited racial divergences which could not be quickly eradicated
by environmental change. The cognitive inferiority of the negro
related to his smaller brain, a physiological disadvantage
difficult to eliminate. Similarly, his lack of spiritual, moral
qualities distanced him by thousands of generations of racial
evolution from the white man, and could not be set to rights within
a realistically conceivable time-scale.

These explanations and the associated evidence were not in
general offered as abstract academic discourses. Haller shows
convincingly how they were intimately bound up with political
debate. They were used to justify disfranchisement, segregation,
forced emigration, even lynch-law. And consistent with what we
would expect of legitimations of such programmes, they applied
'scientific' principles of explanation only to the extent that
they were expedient, and departed from them immediately they
ceased to reinforce appropriate evaluations. Everything was
insistently turned to the disadvantage of the negro; even his
lower than average suicide rate was taken not as evidence of
stability of character, but as an indication of dulled sensi-
bility and a lack of high-mindedness.

Haller leaves us in no doubt of the extent to which explanations of racial differences were shaped by their role as legitimations. He cites the features of negro physiology employed to
assign them a place in the chain of being or the evolutionary
hierarchy. Always, features which put them between apes and white

men were selected; characteristics which would have inverted the
rank order, such as, for example, lip thickness or hair qualities,
were never mentioned in this context. Similarly, the more acute
facial angle of the negro was often cited as evidence of his lower
position in the scheme of things; but nobody who reasoned in
this way ever took the notably steep facial angle of Chinese as an
indication of superiority or even parity with whites. Other
factors were invoked to vilify Chinese. As in specific instances
so it was at the more general level. Hereditarian perspectives,
at this time in the USA, generally stressed the inheritance of
acquired characteristics, and were thus explicitly optimistic
concerning the effects of environmental improvement and ameliora-
tion. When they discussed racial differences, however, writers
became markedly less enthusiastic for the arguments they set such
store by in other contexts. Expediency demanded a pessimistic
analysis of the possibilities of the negro, and writers modified
the character of their hereditarianism in order to provide one.

It is surely appropriate to suggest that Haller has identified
here an ideologically determined stream of thought. We do not
need to examine every individual component of the stream in order
to justify the diagnosis; for the extent to which knowledge reflects concealed interests does not depend upon the proportion
of individual cognitive acts involved in generating and sustaining
it which themselves are determined directly by the interests.
Consider an individual, in the social context discussed by Haller,
who approached the problem of negro-white differences untouched by
illegitimate interests. Such an unlikely individual would not
work in a cultural vacuum. His methods of approach and his
organising concepts would have, to an extent, to be drawn from a
cultural context already shaped by such interests. The body of
existing knowledge upon which he would have to some degree to
rely would be a body of knowledge selected, organised and perhaps
generated in the light of concealed interests. He would find,
for example, extensive tabulations of data demonstrating the
smaller brain size of the negro - impressive material in its own
terms, but interestingly divergent from the empirical findings on
the subject taken to be reliable today. Thus, his work, however
individually commendable and 'disinterested', could not be set
aside as independent of ideological determination. It could still
be treated as part of an overall stream of thought reflecting
the operation of concealed interests.

But, given that a general relationship between knowledge and
illicit interests can properly be asserted, what does it imply
in detail? Certainly it implies that a whole field of knowledge
as it developed in a particular culture over a period of time
deserves to be treated with suspicion. Any knowledge drawn from
the field is deservedly suspect, directly or indirectly, of ideological determination, and hence of not necessarily possessing the
technical or predictive adequacy imputed to it by its proponents. If
a body of knowledge is shown to be ideologically determined as an
institution, its overall credibility as a resource in prediction and
control is called into question.

On the other hand, surprisingly little positive information
is conveyed by the diagnosis. It does not enable us reliably to

make any pronouncements about particular knowledge claims. If we
have not studied them in particular we can say nothing of them in
particular - whether of the way in which they were generated, or how
they were sustained, or of their technical utility, predictive
value or adequacy as measured by whatever test or criterion. Nor
does the diagnosis have much general predictive value with regard
to the future credibility of the field of knowledge as a whole. If
we accept that a body of knowledge is sustained to some extent by
concealed interests, then we would expect its usage and credibility to diminish, or its form to be modified, when the interests
cease to operate. But we should need much more specific and
detailed information before we could say more. In particular, we
should need to ascertain the relative importance of concealed
and legitimate interests, in sustaining knowledge in various
concrete contexts.

When concealed interests cease to operate, any knowledge which
they have previously sustained only tends to lose credibility where
it represents a distortion of what is naturally reasonable in terms
of a legitimate interest in prediction and control. (14) To relate
'ideologies' solely and simply to concealed social interests is to
neglect the extreme pervasiveness of the other great interest in
terms of which knowledge develops, the legitimate interest in
prediction and control. And to neglect this is an even more
serious mistake than to neglect the possible influence of concealed
interests on predominantly 'technical/predictive knowledge'. For
even when knowledge is developed and sustained solely to rational-
ise and legitimate, these very interests are best served by keeping the knowledge in question as close as possible to what is
indicated on more legitimate grounds, since it is on such grounds
that proponents will typically defend the merits of the knowledge
in question. The greater the apparent predictive and technical
efficacy of racial or political 'ideologies' the easier it is to
account them 'scientifically valid'.

This may be an obvious point, but it is an extremely important
one. We now have substantial evidence that ideological determinants have been involved in the growth of scientific knowledge,
and have influenced scientific work which has significantly
contributed to the creation of what we now accept as valid knowledge. It seems clear, for example, that the work of Karl
Pearson's school in statistics was influenced, far more profoundly
than anyone who accepted its validity could have admitted, by
social interests, and in particular a commitment to eugenics
(MacKenzie, 1976). Yet that work generated the resources from
which current statistics, as used by sociologists and many other
groups, was developed. Such ideologically determined material often
proves of continuing value within a predominantly instrumentally
oriented research tradition because it tends, for a variety of
reasons, to deviate minimally from legitimate procedures and
pathways. (15)

On the whole, knowledge does not appear and disappear as various
kinds of interest wax and wane. More often it continues in an
intellectual tradition, as a resource to be deployed in the
furtherance of whatever interests are institutionally predominant.
With this instrumental conception of knowledge one need not be

disturbed by the fact, so worrying to historians of science and so incomprehensible to many epistemologists, that yesterday's 'ideology' frequently transforms itself imperceptibly into today's 'science'.

Empirically, knowledge does seem to have differentiated over time so that its various special fields have come to centre upon particular, narrowly defined, interests. In particular, its scientific wing now experiences the effect of interests in rationalisation in a much attentuated form, and there exists within it knowledge which has become almost entirely dissociated from functions of legitimation and persuasion, and has developed for a considerable period entirely under the impetus of isoteric technical interests. But it is altogether too simple to think of knowledge having differentiated so that science is now geared *solely* to esoteric technical-predictive interests. Although knowledge has doubtless differentiated around diverse interests and goals, the interplay of knowledge as an institution and the two great classes of general interests which bear upon it is too complex to be captured by such a simple formula. Let us illustrate this with one final example.

Euclid's 'Elements' dates, we are told, from 323 BC; and since that time its knowledge has existed as an institution in western cultures. Even today it is still occasionally maintained and transmitted in a form very close to the original. How are we to account for the persistence of this institution over such a long period? It might be thought that the answer is a very simple one: from the instrumentalist perspective of this volume, Euclid establishes relationships of equivalence and properties of figures of enduring predictive and manipulative value in a vast range of human activities. In studying Euclid one gains familiarity with conventions, and competence in operations, of value in the context of a very wide range of cultures. (16)

Let us not deny how important this is as part of the answer to our question. But let us also remember that what has persisted as the institution of Euclidean geometry is more than a set of technical instructions. Euclid offers us a set of theorems and proofs; it is these which have persisted. It might be said that the Euclidean proofs are thought to provide rational grounds for regarding the associated procedures as generally valid or applicable, and that this is why they are sustained. But it is far from obvious that this is so. It is extraordinarily easy to generate doubts about Euclidean proofs. By this I do not mean that it is easy to generate facile sceptical remarks about them, but that with only a little thought one can become genuinely dubious and concerned about their status and scope. Perhaps more to the point, mathematicians have had doubts about the standing of the proofs, both generally and in particular cases. Very commonly, they have objected to the use of diagrams and figures, which if 'wrongly' drawn can lead to 'erroneous' results. (17) There have been attempts to replace this form of proof with completely deductive derivations from 'axioms', or as Forder puts it in his axiomatisation (1927), from 'unproved propositions about undefined entities'. Most mathematicians would probably agree with Forder when he notes that the Euclidean proofs commonly encountered in educational institutions are unsound, even if they did not entirely agree with his own attempt at improvement. (18)

None the less, the original proofs have persisted little modified as institutions and have not been superseded by more properly
'rigorous' constructions. Probably this has been a consequence
of the operation of unacknowledged interests. Pedagogical writings
of many periods have praised the educational value of Euclid, and
noted how 'compelling' his presentation can be made to the mind
of the student. The formal style, and the apparent psychological
power of the diagrams, have been considered valuable reinforce-
ments of the credibility and authority of the teacher; and the
concrete proofs have been taken as readily transmitted general
models of good thinking. (19) There has indeed been a continuing
text-book literature wherein Euclid has been modified (at the
expense of 'rigour' as Forder conceived it) to facilitate pedagogical interests, and perhaps even more general concealed interests
in social control. (20) These works make an *increased* use of
diagrams and seek to deploy those which most memorably exemplify
and 'impose upon the mind' the relationships to be established by
the proofs.

Would then the teaching of plane geometry have departed radically
from the Euclidean style in educational contexts radically different from those traditional in western cultures? Probably so.
It is interesting to note how innovations in modern mathematics
teaching associated with the move to a less authoritarian pedagogy
have involved a movement away from the Euclidean tradition. But,
again, one must beware of overgeneralisation and resist the tempta-
tion to attribute the persistence of the Euclidean style of proof
solely to pedagogical and other unacknowledged interests. Learning the Euclidean proofs has not always been simply a matter of
learning why certain theorems are valid. At times, it has also
been, for some, the learning of a technique for advancing mathematics. Particular Euclidean proofs were also exemplary models
of proofs which could be employed as resources or precedents in
the construction of new theorems and proofs. Learning proofs was
learning how to prove, a legitimate if esoteric interest of the
mathematician himself. Here is another, and probably not the
last important interest to be taken into account in understanding
the distribution of this particular cultural form, and how it
would have been altered at any time by the removal of any of
the interests which were then sustaining it. (21)

As a general rule, it would seem unwise simply to assume the
complete legitimacy of any body of knowledge, however respected
or apparently instrumentally efficacious. However, an institution
wherein knowledge is generated and sustained entirely under the
impetus of legitimate instrumental interests would seem a realistic
and empirically realisable ideal. Knowledge does not *have* to be
ideologically determined, as the term has been used in this chapter.
(And it is perhaps worth recording my personal evaluation, in
opposition to many who apparently hold to the contrary, that knowledge and its production should not be so determined.)

It remains the case that if we generate and sustain knowledge
entirely in terms of authentic interests, we are still obliged
to employ existing knowledge as a resource. And that knowledge
will be the product of a historical development wherein concealed,
illegitimate interests are bound to have been operative. In

some ways, this is a very disturbing fact. As was stated in the
previous chapter, we have no way of demonstrating that learning,
which must start from existing knowledge and conceptualisations,
can generate new knowledge entirely independent of this necessary
given starting point. Hence present knowledge, sustained entirely
as an instrumental resource, possesses, as it were, a suspect
pedigree. Such a conclusion is not, however, quite so depressing
as it might seem. On an instrumental view of knowledge we can
make a profitable analogy with our physical tools and implements.
Our present range of technological resources is clearly to some
extent a consequence of the interests our technology has served
in the past and the functions it has performed. Among these
interests and functions, many will no longer be operative. Yet
they are part of the pedigree of our technology; to some extent
they have determined its present form and range of artefacts, even
though many technological innovations and modifications have been
made since they became redundant. This is because new technology
grows out of old technology, and does not spring up 'ab initio'
in response to new needs and interests.

We do not, however, worry all that much that our technique is
historically conditioned in this way; we can accept that our
transistor circuitry is still recognisable as modified valve
circuitry, or that the latest collapsible children's push-chairs
are modifications of the mechanisms of aircraft undercarriages.
Similarly, with our more abstract knowledge and verbally formulated beliefs, there is no need to give too much concern to their
dubious pedigree, since essentially they are our resources to
use as we find appropriate. Simply by applying them, and modifying
them as we find need in our goal directed activity, we serve our
interests as well as we can.

Chapter 3

THE PROBLEM OF IMPUTATION

1 TWO CONTRASTING SOLUTIONS

Whether and how thought or belief can be attributed to social classes, or other formations, as the consequences of their particular interests, constitutes the problem of imputation in the sociology of knowledge (cf. Child, 1941). When it was first considered by sociologists and historical materialists, they built upon the hypothesis that the contrasting concepts, beliefs and overall styles of thought of different social classes were intelligible entirely in terms of their different interests and objective positions in the social structure; thought was effectively made a direct function of social interest. And, indeed, this simplest possible initial hypothesis provided an excellent starting point for investigation of the imputation problem. It inspired empirical work, and prompted attempts to analyse and clarify key concepts such as 'class' and 'interest'.

None the less, it was soon acknowledged that such a simple hypothesis did not satisfactorily relate beliefs and interests as they actually existed. Despite wide-ranging disagreements upon what constituted a class, its interests and its beliefs, all investigators were able to agree that simple direct correspondences between these various entities as empirical phenomena could not be convincingly established. Beliefs which seemed rationally indicated by the interests of one class were found to be disturbingly common among the members of another; the dominant beliefs of a class were sometimes extraordinarily resistant to being made rationally intelligible in terms of any plausible version of its objective interests; sometimes so much diversity of belief and thought was found within a class as to preclude analysis of what were the dominant forms. Historical materialists were particularly aware of problems with the thought of the working class, which seemed peculiarly liable to manifestations of resignation, apathy, acquiescence in exploitation, or even respect and admiration for those higher in the social order.

On the other hand, it was still reasonable, on the basis of what had been empirically revealed, to hold that some relationship existed between beliefs, interests and social structure.

To hold that their relationship was random was altogether less plausible than the admittedly unsatisfactory hypothesis previously adhered to. The problem of imputation remained a real, empirically based, matter for investigation; what was needed was a more sophisticated treatment of it. Historical materialists tended to respond to this need by retaining their basic concepts of class and interest, and coupling them to evidence less directly than before by use of more elaborated and speculative theorising. In contrast, those with an empiricist orientation in the sociology of knowledge moved away from heavily theory-laden terms like 'class' to categories which they found easier to map onto distinctive clusters of thought and belief.

Lukács's approach to the imputation problem (1923) is a good example of the first strategy. As we have already noted, he imputed an 'ideal class-consciousness' to every social class, on the basis of its real interests. This ideal consciousness represented the most rational thought of which that class was capable; it was what participants in the class would think and believe when they gained full awareness of the world (natural and social) and their own position within it. In this limiting case, thought was logically implied by real interests; here only the particular real interests of a class would limit the scope of its understanding and thus maintain a degree of 'false-consciousness' in its thought.

The imputed ideal consciousness of a class could not, however, be expected even roughly to resemble what its members actually thought and believed at any particular time. Such empirically ascertainable beliefs would be held by men with limited awareness, living in societies where others had an interest in restricting their vision and distorting their consciousness. What men actually believed was an indication, not necessarily of their class and interests, but of the existence of limitations acting upon their experience to obscure their awareness of their real interests and restrict the exercise of their rationality. For any class, a set of hypothesised relationships was held to exist as follows:

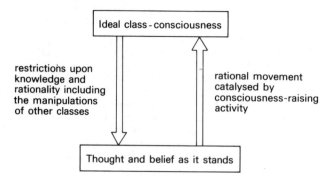

Figure 3.1

Thus, Lukács's account preserved the logical relationship of thought and interest from empirical disconfirmation, but at the cost of reducing its empirical significance. The ideal forms of

consciousness which are logically determined by interest cannot
any longer be identified by empirical methods. They do not correspond to existing forms of consciousness, and Lukács offers us no
other means of ascertaining their characteristics. Evidently, we
are in no position to have knowledge of them. And since existing
thought must be explained in terms of its divergence from an
ideal form of consciousness, we evidently cannot hope to explain
existing thought either.

Hence, formally, there is some justice in the charge often made
against Lukács, that in seeking to protect important tenets of
historical materialism from refutation he banished them to the
realm of metaphysics. In practice, however, one should not condemn Lukács's work as a mass of metaphysical speculation and ignore
its many concrete claims. Take, for example, his discussion of
the gap between actual and ideal consciousness. This gap, he
asserted, is likely to vary in magnitude among the different
social classes. In a given society, the ruling class will be
least restricted in vision by circumstances or the machinations
of other classes. Its members will, in the course of becoming predominant, have organised themselves and participated in the
revolutionary activity necessary to their own success; such
activity is precisely what generates real awareness of one's society
and one's class position therein. Hence, the actual consciousness of a ruling class is likely to be close to its ideal class-
consciousness, and stable over time, whatever 'consciousness-
raising' events occur; it can reasonably be characterised as
inherently bourgeois, for example, if the ruling class is
bourgeois. With exploited classes, on the other hand, or incip-
ient rising ones such as the proletariat, actual consciousness will
diverge widely from the ideal. What is predicted here is that
consciousness raising by dialectically aware élites, constantly
urging struggle and revolutionary activity, will move the thought
of a class closer and closer to the imputed ideal consciousness.
Similarly the experience of life and activity in society can
itself at times tend to broaden the vision of an exploited class,
particularly at times when class oppositions become polarised and
circumstances of intense conflict arise. On both counts, the overall consciousness of a class can be increased by the activities
of particularly aware minority groups.

Its use in analysis of this kind suggests that, whatever its
formal deficiencies, Lukács's theory deserves to be treated as a
concrete account of existing distributions of thought and belief,
and the likely course of their development. It is, moreover, an
account which possesses two important merits. First, it continues
to relate knowledge to social structure, and specifically to one
of the most significant and dynamic theories of social structure.
Second, in common with most variants of historical materialism,
but unlike some current sociological theories, it does not make
the untenable assumption that men's activity can be predicted
entirely from what they say, or even from what they believe.
Instead, it builds the fact that man is forever developing and
modifying his thought and belief, right into its basic structure.
Rather than assuming that man must understand his circumstances
in terms of his existing beliefs and ideas, it stresses that

those beliefs and ideas may very well be modified by circumstances.

Unfortunately, Lukács's conceptions of how socially structured interests constrain knowledge, and how practice develops and extends it, are both utterly misconceived. And in both cases the misconception is rooted in the notion of 'ideal class-consciousness'. Let us take first Lukács's account of the way a class's real interests constrain its ideal consciousness; this is found in his discussion of 'bourgeois thought'. This thought, as we have said, is held to be very close to its ideal state, to the point where its rational extension is restricted only by real bourgeois interests, and where it accordingly can be seen as logically determined by those interests. How, then, is this determination empirically manifested? According to Lukács, its interests prevent the bourgeoisie becoming aware of certain 'contradictions' in its own thought. It is, for example, incapable of recognising the contradiction between the freedom stressed as the right of all in its polemics and ideology, and the exploitation which is the lot of the proletariat under capitalism. To recognise this contradiction would be 'morally intolerable'; it would result in the self-confidence of the bourgeoisie evaporating, its will to maintain its predominance slackening, and hence its downfall.

It is clear that Lukács's notion of 'logical determination' is very different from that current in the Anglo-Saxon academic world, but let us not hold that against him. The basic criticism to be made of his logical, or psychological, thesis, is that it involves assumptions about how people think and act quite breathtaking in their extent, yet entirely lacking the support of argument or concrete evidence. We surely do not know enough about ourselves or our own history to permit ourselves the luxury of assumptions of this kind. Indeed, what evidence there is suggests that neither the 'bourgeois class' in particular, nor human collectivities generally, possess the moral delicacy or the tendency to cognitive ossification which is here imputed to them.

The inadequacy of Lukács's account of the dynamic character of knowledge has already been pointed out. Instead of attempting to examine how existing knowledge is modified by men in response to perceived needs and problems, he arbitrarily assumed that in the course of unconstrained activity consciousness moved forward towards some ideal state. Hence he overlooked the dependence of new knowledge upon old; in an important sense he failed to treat the generation of new knowledge and new modes of thought as an ongoing historical process.

Instead, he was content to assert what is essentially a teleological conception of the growth of knowledge, with an ideal form of consciousness as 'telos'. This led him into an oft-noted formal difficulty whenever he attempted to account for or evaluate existing thought. In doing so, he was obliged to cite its deviations from the ideal form; but by his own account, he, Lukács, could neither trust his own consciousness to produce reliable knowledge of them, nor hope to have access to ideal forms of consciousness so as to know them. His discussions of class-consciousness suggest that Lukács surged ahead of the rest of humanity, on a dialectical thought-wave, to return with the

knowledge of a future epoch.   There is, however, no reason why
we ourselves should credit Lukács with having performed this feat,
or subscribe to his teleology.   Rather we should acknowledge that
the notion of ideal forms of consciousness, being teleological, is
incompatible with a naturalistic orientation to the sociology of
knowledge, and that, accordingly, Lukács's ideas cannot serve as
a basis for solving the problem of imputation.

The maximum possible contrast with Lukács's approach can be
obtained by examining work which embodies a piecemeal, empiricist
approach to beliefs.   A recent book which embodies these tendencies in an extreme form is Lewis Feuer's 'Ideology and the
Ideologists' (1975).   Since its presuppositions are clearly apparent,
and underlie other empiricist writings, it is worth examining in
some detail how it deals with problems of imputation. (1)

Unlike Lukács, Feuer is concerned only with those particular
systems of thought and belief he calls 'ideologies', and does not
seek to relate the entire corpus of belief of any group or stratum
to its interests or social position.   Indeed, he regards social
factors as irrelevant to the explanation of the incidence of
scientifically valid beliefs.   He takes a restricted unsymmetrical
view of the sociology of knowledge and would probably think it
better called the sociology of error;   social factors distort
beliefs so that they no longer deserve to be treated as knowledge.
The problem of imputation is associated with a limited range of
beliefs only - 'ideologies'.

'Ideologies' are composite systems of ideas.   Central to any
such system is a 'Mosaic myth', which expounds the role of
intellectual leaders in effecting some aim or mission of cosmological significance and indubitable moral worth.   This generally involves advancing the cause of some selected class, race,
nationality or other 'oppressed' collectivity, with which the
intellectual leaders identify themselves.   Besides the central myth
and the chosen mission, the ideology contains a justification of
the mission and demonstration of its feasibility;   this requires
the organisation of philosophical principles, general conceptions
of nature and society, and empirical claims, into a coherent overall world view or cosmology.

Such composite constructions, or 'ideologies', are held by
Feuer to be imputable only to the small groups of intellectuals
who characteristically profess and advocate them. (2)   They both
express the ambitions of these groups, and serve as instruments
in their attempts to fulfil that ambition.   This is why they exist,
and why they remain limited in distribution to intellectual
élites;   the groups with whom the élites identify are normally
found to be unmoved by the rhetoric of their champions, and to
operate upon the basis of more piecemeal and pragmatic beliefs.
The working class, in particular, is typically indifferent to
'ideology'.

The 'ideologies' of the intellectuals are not to be understood
as genuine attempts to understand the world, however limited;   they
are not conjectural responses to curiosity, but expedient responses to practical and emotional desires and interests.   As
such, 'ideologies' are not total thought systems, representing the
vision of reality of any group, or the perspective of any section

of society. Rather they are constructed to fit with other extant
beliefs and ideas in such a way as to be persuasive; they are no
more than parts connected with other parts of a wider culture.
Ideologists may, for example, adopt a scientistic philosophy to
exploit the high credibility of science in a culture, or conversely,
irrationalism, to gain the support of elements in society opposed
to scientific expertise and bureaucratic controls.

Thus, in so far as he treats of 'ideologies', Feuer can be
regarded as an instrumentalist, who talks of ideas as tools employed
for certain ends in a particular social context. Hence, he holds
that there can be no necessary connections between ideas and
particular groups or classes; 'ideologies' will bolster themselves with the currently most effective ideas and philosophies,
and, generally, these will be the most fashionable ones. When
science is the rage, cases are best made by appeal to science;
when nationalism is strong the 'spirit of the nation' is appropriately referred to - and so on. Feuer provides extensive evidence
for his claims here, showing how the same ideas have been employed
for opposed purposes at different times by different groups of
ideologists. He traces, for example, the evolution of Kantian
philosophy from a radical bourgeois weapon, used to attack the
established German moral order, to a rightist dogma utilised in
defending traditional religion and rule. Similarly he notes how
the 'bourgeois ideology' of utilitarianism was taken up by Utopian
sociologists, and later even by out-and-out conservative thinkers.
And analogous developments are shown to have occurred with pragmatism, positivism, idealism, and a number of other doctrines.

Feuer accounts for the rise and fall of 'ideologies' by an idiosyncratic blending of psychological explanation in terms of
emotions and desires, and explanation in terms of the clash of
generations or age-groups. When a new or revived philosophy comes
into prominence, and is used by group after group of intellectuals
to validate their cause, it eventually becomes an orthodoxy. But
any such set of ideas will lay stress on some aspects of the psyche
at the expense of others; its acceptance will inevitably involve
the repression of some emotion or other: determinism, for example,
will repress the desire for spontaneity, but irrationalist reactions to it will repress the desire for order. Hence in the
triumph of any such position the seeds of its overthrow are planted;
the repressed emotions will burst forth and find expression in a
reaction to the ideological orthodoxy. The instrument of this
resurgence is the youngest rising generation of intellectuals. To
them, the existing ideas represent the prestige and authority of
an earlier generation, whose prominence obstructs their own rise.
To them, deviant ideas can be used to analyse the inadequacies and
one-sidedness of existing orthodoxies, and to develop a challenge
to the existing structure of intellectual authority. Thus, ideological change is normally brought about by generational revolt;
deviant young intellectuals differentiate themselves by their
association with some appropriate heresy, and from that position
lead an attack upon their elders. If they succeed, then their
new doctrine rapidly spreads, until the conditions for a new
generational revolt become established.

The details of this particular account of the dissemination of

'ideologies' will not be evaluated here, where only the merits and
drawbacks of its general features will be considered. Indubitably,
one important merit is the concern to understand beliefs as they
actually exist and are distributed. If Feuer's explanatory
hypotheses are wrong, at least they relate to existing phenomena
and are thus vulnerable to concrete testing and open to empirical
feedback of a direct, immediate kind. And if his evidence is
sound and properly representative, it is material which should be
of value to any approach within the sociology of knowledge, however theoretically sophisticated.

There are indeed obvious weaknesses and superficialities in
Feuer's treatment of concrete material. But it does suffice to
show that postulated 'logical' connections between beliefs and
interests are of no empirical relevance, and to support an instrumental, context-mediated account of the connection such as his
own. This explanation, which treats the components of 'ideologies'
essentially as tools, assembled to further the aims or interests of
groups of ideologists, has clear empirical implications. It can
be checked, and to some extent Feuer does so, by reference to the
actual distribution of 'ideologies' in society, and by observation of the circumstances under which they are abandoned, modified
or diffused.

In addition, the notion of beliefs and ideas as tools is a
metaphor which facilitates awareness of their historical dimension.
Just as our choice of a tool will depend upon the context in which
we wish to use it, and upon the range of tools from which we can
choose, so the choice of beliefs or ideas will depend upon the
context and the available resources. In this case, however, the
context is the existing social situation, and the resources are the
concepts and ideas available, or readily synthesisable, for incor-
poration into the systems of legitimation that Feuer calls 'ideologies'. The dependence which this implies of men's thinking upon
the thinking of their predecessors, even upon thinking they reasonably believe themselves to have transcended and overthrown, is
surely incontrovertible. Marx seems to have taken some such
dependence for granted, and was perfectly ready to acknowledge his
debt to the political economists; but, in practice, the topic has
been neglected in the development of historical materialism. We
have seen how Lukács, who tirelessly railed against positivism and
empiricism for their neglect of historical processes, and whose
Hegelianism might have made him particularly sensitive to this
point, failed to take real account of it in developing his theory
of imputation. Ironically, although he makes little or nothing
of the point himself, Feuer's instrumentalism allows beliefs and
ideologies to be situated more clearly and firmly in the context
of historical change.

In thus outlining the most important merits of his work, however,
we have put ourselves in a good position from which to examine its
weaknesses and limitations. Its instrumentalism, for all its
plausibility, remains a partial theory, applicable only to 'ideologies'. Science, and everyday empirical knowledge, are accounted
for by a separate theory, in terms of their correspondence with
reality. But this division is not the result of detailed investigation of both kinds of belief; it simply expresses a set of a priori

evaluations: esteemed beliefs are accounted for by a correspondence
theory, despised beliefs by an instrumental theory. Moreover, the
notions of correspondence, in terms of which scientific and other
rational empirical beliefs are justified, are never elucidated.
Feuer is never less empirical, never more prone to romantic mytho-
logising, than when discussing 'empirical science' or 'scientific
method'. His simplistic references to science, and his extraordinarily confident invocations of the long-rejected justifications
of it current half a century ago would seem to stand condemned by
his own standards as components of his 'ideology'. Thus, whilst his
instrumentalist conception of 'ideologies', with its rejection of
'correspondences' between beliefs or ideas and social groups,
deserves sympathetic consideration, the general framework in which
it is set does not.

Nor is the particular form taken by his instrumentalism acceptable as it stands. It treats beliefs and ideas as isolated units,
which can be wrapped up and posted from context to context with
their meanings attached, as it were, as part of the package. This
misconception often arises from the atomistic, individualistic
tendencies characteristic of much empiricist thought, but it is
manifest in an extreme form in Feuer's work. When he talks of
utilitarianism or Kantianism or pragmatism, he tends to treat them
as things, unchanged as they move from context to context, either
in their verbal forms or in the meaning attributable to those
forms; Feuer is content to refer to them as 'philosophical unit-
ideas' and to imagine them undergoing as little change as bricks
undergo when transported on a lorry.

In fact, even the most superficial examination of any of these
traditions should suffice to expose the problems of such an
approach. Just how we can demonstrate 'the same idea' to be
present in different contexts, even when identical words and formulations are used, is a source of continuing difficulty; (3) it
would be ludicrous, for example, to imagine that everyone who
employed the notion of 'utility', even say in nineteenth-century
Britain, had 'the same thing' in mind. We need to remember the
essential continuity of cultural forms, the dependence of later
upon earlier, whilst simultaneously remaining aware of the fluid,
negotiable character of all meanings. Accounts of knowledge and
culture which do this satisfactorily are still in a very early
stage of development. (4) But Feuer's theory, which reifies and
atomises ideas, is glaringly inadequate.

Any satisfactory account of concepts or ideas must recognise
that their meaning is either determined by, or more or less equivalent to, their use; hence it depends upon their context of use
and their relationship in use to other concepts. This does not
involve renunciation of the instrumental analogy of ideas with
tools. It indicates the way in which this analogy should be
exploited. Since to borrow an idea is always to borrow a whole
set of interrelated terms understood in terms of their existing
applications, it should be understood that what is borrowed is not
a thing but a pattern, a complex of cultural elements. An idea
thus conceived, borrowed as a tool or resource out of another
context, does not bring its use/meaning along with itself intact,
as it were sticking to the complex like a label. Rather, by

virtue of the new uses to which it is put in the new context,
and the new referents and connections with other concepts which
it acquires, it takes on a different meaning, even if this is
generally recognisably related to its previous one.

Feuer's tendency to individualistic, atomistic forms of thought
also adversely influences his conceptualisation of society. It
is perfectly possible to use a term like 'élite' in a structural
rather than an aggregational sense; one can talk of élite roles,
for example, or the expectations and pressures which élites encounter in different institutional settings. There is disagreement
about what we can validly indicate by the use of notions like
'institution' or 'social structure', but from practically any standpoint the term 'élite' can be given a structural or sociological
significance. Feuer, however, insistently treats élites as aggre-
gates of particular autonomous individuals, and their thought and
behaviour as a collective-psychological phenomenon entirely intelligible in terms of individual emotions and motivations. Elites
are characterised as manipulators of society, but not as part of it.
The possibility that such élites are defined as élites by their
audience is ignored; the likelihood that the motives of their
members, which account for their ideologies, are themselves the
products of more general social factors is never properly taken
into account; the concentration of 'ideology' in particular institutional contexts is mentioned in passing as the by-product of the
generational conflict in which new ideologies arise. Feuer has no
sense of social structure.

Hence it is not surprising that we find immense gaps in his
account. If young intellectuals are egotistically motivated by the
desire for success and power, why do they not all express the most
expedient 'ideology', given the circumstances of their time? Why
do they instead spread across a wide range of 'ideologies' including some obviously inexpedient ones? One possible answer is that
'ideologists' think and act authentically as members of larger
social formations, occupying diverse social roles, being committed to the fortunes of different groups, and seeking different
bases of support. Their diverse 'ideologies' would then have a
real basis in social divisions and stratifications. Such an account
would relate the spectrum of 'ideologies' to the structure of
society as a whole, a move which Feuer appears to be unable or
unwilling to make. Yet it is hard to see how some such move, whatever its specific nature, can be avoided, if a full understanding
of the variation and distribution of 'ideologies' is to be
obtained.

A similar omission of essential references to social structure
is apparent in Feuer's account of ideological change. He asserts
that élites modify their 'ideologies' along lines indicated by
personal expediency. But, to understand such changes, we need to
understand the social factors which determine what is expedient.
Take, for example, the changes in Bolshevik thought and practice
which followed the 1917 revolution. Certainly these were not
'logical' extensions of earlier Bolshevik principles. They do
indeed make good sense as expedient adaptations to circumstances
by a political élite with but a tenuous grasp of political power
and little real control over their country. Its members adapted

their programmes to actual contingencies. They adjusted their
'ideology' on such matters as the role of money, the importance
of 'workers'-control', or the class position of peasantry, so that
it implied, 'ex post facto', that what had already happened and what
seemed necessarily about to happen was what *ought* to happen. They
skilfully rode with the political tide. But precisely because of
this, because they expediently adapted their 'ideology', that 'ideology' and its development was being influenced by social structural
factors. The exigiencies of political practice which brought about
ideological adaptation were in turn determined by such factors as
social reactions to Bolshevik policies, and thus ultimately by interests and their social distribution. Unlike Lukács, who at least
attempted to account for changes of this kind, Feuer simply fails to
deal with such matters, and assumes that expediency is in some way
self-explanatory. Clearly, his particular brand of empiricism is no
more capable of sustaining a sociological approach to knowledge than
was Lukács's teleology.

2 THE PROBLEM RECONSIDERED

If the patterns of distribution of beliefs and interests in society
were both isomorphous with the social structure, there would be no
continuing problem of imputation in the sociology of knowledge. If
beliefs, interests and social structure were totally uncorrelated,
there would likewise be no such problem, since the perspectives
within which it arose would never have been adopted. In fact, the
three variables do frequently seem to be related, but in a complex
and apparently unsystematic way.

   Lukács attempted to sort out the relationship by assuming that
social structure determined real interests and their distribution.
He then postulated that under ideal conditions interests logically
determined thought and belief. Unfortunately, this last postulate
could, at best, only be used in very special circumstances to link
beliefs to interests, and thus account for the thought of people by
reference to their objective social situations. And its alleged
utility as an indicator of likely changes in beliefs and modes of
thought, which Lukács regarded as more important than its applicability to existing thought, was inferred from a completely untenable
set of presuppositions.

   The general empiricist perspective adopted by Feuer is just as unsatisfactory. It takes a contemplative view of knowledge and treats
aims, desires, interests, or any other goal-orienting properties of
actors as nothing more than likely sources of bias and distortion.
Certain features of his account are, nonetheless, worth further
consideration. He starts with particular sets of beliefs or concepts
which appear to be associated with particular believers or groups
of believers, and he asks why the association is found.
This is an excellent down-to-earth starting point: an explanation is sought for an observed correlation. And Feuer's suggested explanation, although unsatisfactory in many ways, has some
important merits. It accounts for beliefs particular to certain
believers by citing causes which are also particular to them - their
particular aims, desires, or interests. (5) And it links cause and

effect by the plausible claim that beliefs are generated and sustained because in a given context they are the most expedient formulations for furthering or legitimating particular aims and interests.

Moreover, the general weaknesses of Feuer's overall framework are
not of great significance when it is only problems of imputation
which are at issue. They lead him into major errors it is true, but
only, in general, with regard to knowledge which it is pointless in
any case to impute to any particular social formation. Thus modern
natural science, the knowledge of which is not predominantly determined by expedient social interests, should certainly not be idealised
and set without the scope of sociological explanation as Feuer does,
but there is scant justification for imputing it to any particular
social formation, even if the imputation is limited to a particular
time and context; scientific knowledge is sustained by widely distributed instrumental interests. Conversely, where expedient social
interests are of major importance, the beliefs and modes of thought
in question will generally more or less conform to Feuer's definition
of an 'ideology', and hence be imputable, in a particular period and
context, to the group whose expedient interests are involved. (6)

Where Feuer goes more significantly astray is in persistently
ignoring social structure. He assumes that the only interests,
motives or emotions relevant to the understanding of beliefs are those
of the believers themselves, considered as individuals, or, for purposes of economic presentation, as groups of individuals. And he
sees no need for any further systematic account of these interests
in terms of social factors.

A concrete instance has already been cited to illustrate just how
groundless and improbable these individualistic assumptions are, but
let us press the point home with a more general counter-example,
particular apposite given Feuer's account of how beliefs are expediently generated and sustained. Consider the various areas in modern
society where there is held to exist a 'market' for beliefs and
ideas: various areas of 'popular culture' and 'youth culture' might
be cited, or perhaps, the 'academic marketplace'. It is surely the
case that much of the material generated for distribution in such
markets is tailored to demand. Its nature may in a sense be related
to the interest of the supplier in satisfying the market, but basically it is the interests of purchasers to which it is best imputed,
and which account for its content. Suppliers will distribute any
beliefs for which there is demand; they are best considered as a
part of the market mechanism, mediating between interests and the
beliefs which those interests call into being. This is but one of
many kinds of situation where the effect of social organisation is
to sustain circuitous connections between beliefs and interests.
Thus, to insist upon imputing beliefs only to those who profess them
is arbitrary, and to explain them in terms which take no formal
cognisance of the status of believers as social actors is simply
incorrect.

Feuer evidently values his restrained individualistic form of explanation as following the precedent of explanation in the natural
sciences. It is a misconception of science he shares with Lukács.
In fact, if we place any value upon scientific precedent, it should
incline us to social-structural explanation as readily as to individualistic forms. (7) And it clearly demonstrates that structural

explanation can be empirically grounded as readily as any other
form; there need be nothing speculative or metaphysical about
structural explanation.

Suppose one were to take the ends of a stick in one's hands, and
snap it in two; a mechanistic account of this event would not base
itself upon any alleged idiosyncracies in the molecules of the wood
at the break point, or insist upon a defect being present there.
Typically a structural explanation would be professed, showing how
the point of fracture was situated relative to the rest of the stick
lying between the hands. The fracture point would be accounted
such, not because of its own properties, but because of its position
in an overall mechanical system. Similarly, if a tube were filled
with liquid and the pressure measured at a given point therein, this
would not be the pressure of a particular piece of liquid, or group
of molecules thereof; it would be a property attributable to a
particular position in a physical system, something unattributable
to any identifiable piece of matter, or atom, or individual.

Such properties are, it is true, always manifested by individual
entities. In the first case above, any particular observed break
will always occur across a particular piece of matter, a particular
identifiable part of the stick. In the second case, any particular
measurement of pressure could plausibly and meaningfully be attributed to the motions of particular molecules in the liquid. System
properties, we could say, are expressed in particular cases by individual entities, to which they are, nonetheless, not meaningfully
attributable. Analogously, features of beliefs may be thought of as
properties of a system embodying interests; they will always be
expressed, and thus made observable, by particular believers, but
should not on that account be considered properties of the believers
rather than of the system itself.

The use of a concept of social structure is sometimes criticised
as reification, as the invention of a thing which determines people's
behaviour from the outside, within which people are, as it were,
trapped, when there is no justification whatsoever for imagining
that any such entity exists. It may be that some uses of the concept of social structure are justly criticised in this way, but the
term need no more be given this interpretation than the physical
structures already referred to need be conceived of as things existing within material objects. To consider entities in structural
terms is normally a strategy employed to draw attention to properties
their constituents possess, not by virtue of their inherent nature
but because of their relationships with other constituents. When
actors are conceptualised as operating within a social structure,
the usual intention is to relate their behaviour to cognitive maps,
expectations, aims and interests possessed by *others,* and projected
upon them because they are perceived as instances of this or that
social category. The social structure is no more the thing that
determines people's behaviour in society than pressure is the thing
that determines the behaviour of molecules in a liquid. In some
contexts pressure is best thought of as the consequence of the
behaviour of the molecules in a liquid. Yet the movement of the
liquid, as some of it, is sometimes well accounted for in terms of
pressure, as when, for example, it spurts from a hole in its containing vessel.

Hence, the imputation of beliefs, via interests, to acceptable social-structural categories, is a procedure which avoids the obvious problems of Feuer's individualism, without any necessary corresponding loss of empirical relevance or testability, or any retreat into reifying mataphysics. (8)   Such structural imputations predict that the form, distribution and influence of beliefs will vary with social structural changes, and this is the basis upon which they can be empirically checked.   They cannot be directly checked, like Feuer's individualistic imputations perhaps could be, by counting how many individuals of different kinds adhere to a particular belief or employ a particular concept. (9)

Those systems of thought and belief which Feuer identifies as ideologies would seem to be best accounted for on the hypothesis that they are associated with constellations of particular interests residing in and patterned by the social structure.   If such systems are used to legitimate particular interests, if these interests are supported by activities and rewards emanating from certain ultimate sources in the social structure, and if social structural change indicates co-variation between the incidence of these sources and the associated interests and beliefs, then each separate finding is evidence in favour of the hypothesis.   On the other hand, some kinds of evidence which have been thought to be essential in assessing imputations within the sociology of knowledge are not of central significance for a structural hypothesis.   In particular, the number or proportion of individuals in a group who hold to a belief ceases to be crucial, as does any correlation between the social origins of individuals and their beliefs.   And the existence of atypical individuals possessing modes of thought or sets of beliefs which diverge from their current interests or past social experiences ceases to be in any way problematic.   The obvious fact that no sociological theory can expect to predict the beliefs of a particular individual is built right into the form of the structural hypothesis.

This is not to say that the distribution of beliefs across individual believers will be random.   It is plausible that, given the nature of known societies, beliefs sustained by particular interests will be associated with the occupants of the social roles which are connected with those interests.   And since individuals with different social origins have differential access to many roles, origins too will likely be associated with particular kinds of belief.   But in the last analysis such relationships are no more than contingent correlations, generated as the structure of interests evokes a range of 'ideologies' in a particular social context.

Thus, when the sociologist of knowledge relates features of the content and distribution of beliefs to interests, and thence to social structure, he should not rest his case upon the evidence of head-counts or prosopography, although they can at times provide useful circumstantial support.   Rather, he should display what the beliefs are evidently used to legitimate and held to imply, and hence what particular interests they apparently serve.   And he should also reveal whether any other factors, of whatever kind, would continue to sustain the beliefs, as distributed, in the absence of the cited interests.   It is upon evidence of this kind,

upon large-scale observation of the temporal co-variation of
beliefs, interests and social structure, and upon the credentials
of his theory of social structure, that the main weight of his
argument is bound to rest.

In conclusion, it will be apparent that the standpoint adopted
here implies a much weaker connection between knowledge and social
structure than that normally asserted by writings in the sociology
of knowledge tradition. A connection between knowledge and interest
is asserted to be sure, but not an internal, logical one. Rather,
it is claimed that interests inspire the construction of knowledge
out of available cultural resources in ways which are specific to
particular times and situations and their overall social and
cultural contexts. As for the relationship of interests and social
structure, it is accepted that some interests are indeed structurally generated and ultimately attributable to social-structural
categories; and individualistc criticisms of structural explanations are held to be misconceived. But no general theory which
sets even particular social interests into direct correspondence
with classes or other categories is assumed or advocated. The way
in which the distribution of particular interests in society is
linked to the social structure is not a matter upon which this
work can make any positive pronouncements. It seems unlikely,
however, that such simple, rigid accounts as that of Lukacs are an
adequate basis for dealing with what is evidently an exceedingly
complex relationship. (10)

It follows from this position that there is a certain very
restricted sense in which thought or belief can be characterised
as that of some social-structural category - a class, occupation,
ethnic group, or whatever. But such imputations are weak in
significance and limited to a particular context. Certainly, they
do not permit beliefs, representations or modes of thought to be
assigned to this or that social class, as it were, by inspection.
Nor do they lead to any predictions about what a particular social
class is capable or incapable of embodying in its consciousness.
These limitations, however, will only count as such to those who
wish to retain unmodified the traditional form of the sociology of
knowledge wherein the problem of imputation was central. From
the present perspective the problem is not, in fact, of great importance. What should be central to the sociology of knowledge is
investigation of the processes whereby knowledge is generated and
sustained in the light of particular situated interests by use of
available cultural resources. It is ironical that a field so much
influenced by historical materialism has instead tended to conceive
of its task as the classification of blocks of knowledge (say as
'bourgeois') very much as if they were objects or things.

3 CONCRETE EXAMPLES

Although detailed appraisal of empirical materials is not possible
here, it is still worth citing concrete cases to give substance to
the foregoing arguments and to exemplify the general points which
have been made. In both the instances selected ample concrete
historical material is available, through which further exploration

of the issues involved could be undertaken.

First, let us consider the scientific controversy concerning the character of human heredity and evolution which occurred in the early years of this century between the 'biometricians' and the 'Mendelians' (cf. MacKenzie and Barnes, 1975). The former group, of whom Karl Pearson was the most notable protagonist, believed that evolution occurred solely by the selection of small 'continuous' differences engendered because the individuals in a population would, with respect to any particular characteristic, distribute themselves normally around some mean value for the characteristic. Thus, a population would only increase in average height because of the differential selection of those individuals in the normal distribution of heights who were slightly taller than the mean. The Mendelians, on the other hand, held that evolution could be discontinuous, that major qualitative individual differences could be passed on without blending into each other and forming con- tinuous ranges of individual properties, and that unpredictable 'saltations' (the results as we would now say of major 'mutations') were always liable to occur. As far as William Bateson, the leader of the Mendelian school in Britain, was concerned, the height of a population might increase suddenly and discontinuously through changes of this sort.

This was a prolonged controversy, and an extremely complex one with many ramifications. Each side possessed an elaborated theory and a characteristic set of methods and techniques; and they clashed over far more issues than the one set out above. (11) None the less, the argument of MacKenzie and Barnes is that the points outlined above were central, and that a number of other matters of dispute were essentially derivative of them. Pearson and the biometricians regarded evolution as a predictable and con- trollable process proceeding by the selection of continuous differ- ences. Bateson and his supporters held a theory wherein the existence of unpredictable, discontinuous mutations was an essential tenet.

In the case of a scientific controversy, technical factors and esoteric professional interests must always be looked to first as a source of explanation. But in the present instance no sufficient basis for the dispute can thereby be found. The opposed forces did not have access to different kinds of evidence with conflicting implications, nor were differences in their training, and in the skills and competences they possessed and valued, of such magni- tude and significance as to account for their different theoretical perspectives. (12) Nothing in the esoteric scientific context satisfactorily accounts for the controversy. Nor was there any technical reason why the disputants should not have agreed to await further evidence, or accepted that both their accounts might have had merit and applied to different kinds of evolutionary change.

Things begin to become clearer however when we turn to the wider social context and the interests set within it. The biometrical view of heredity and evolution was deployed as an accessory and legitimation of eugenics, a programme for the gradual 'improvement of the race' by deliberate modification of the relative fertility of the various groups in society. The eugenic programme, which was most readily justified if evolution was a predictable process, amenable to gradual redirection by the cumulative effects of

continuing small-scale interventions, was one manifestation of
the reformist, interventionist strands of thinking associated with
the rising professional middle class (MacKenzie, 1976) It was
actively supported by Pearson and many of his followers, who developed biometrical techniques with its problems explicitly in
mind.

The dominant trend of industrialisation engendered professional
roles as a response to problems of administration and control, so
that the interests of the new professional class were firmly bound
to the existing pattern of gradual social change or 'progress', and
to the arising new industrial order. But advocacy of the laissez-
faire doctrines popular with industrialists and manufacturers would
have been inexpedient for the professional class, whose raison
d'être was to intervene in social processes and manage and manipulate them on the basis of its supposed expertise. Elitist forms of
'socialism' or other interventionist policies were more apposite,
along with scientistic celebrations of the reliability and potency of
expert knowledge. Eugenics embodied doctrines of this kind together
with a more particular appeal: it identified a problem - the low
fitness of the 'race' and particularly of its lowest segment, the
'residuum' of the destitute and unemployed - and offered professional skills and esoteric knowledge to dominant groups as the means
of overcoming this problem. Professional-scientific skills were
displayed as valuable resources for the ruling class; and if the
discrimatory policies of 'positive' eugenics or the compulsory
prevention of breeding implied by 'negative' eugenics aroused the
hostility of the 'residuum', the powerless bottom layer of society,
there was nothing to fear from that.

In short, eugenics can be regarded as one of the ideologically
determined modes of thought characteristic of the rising professional middle class in the context of English society in the period
1890-1910, and intelligible in terms of its particular social
interests. (13) And many of the controversial features of the related biometrical knowledge and technique as it stood at this time
can likewise be imputed to the operation of these particular interests. If we wish to understand the content of biometrical knowledge
we have to make reference to the social structure at the most
general level.

Although the evidence is less clearcut, and will not be discussed here, it would seem that the vigour with which the controversial claims of biometry were opposed and countered by the British
Mendelians should also be related to social structure. Dogmatic
stress on discontinuity and unpredictability in evolution can
be linked with conservative opposition to industrialisation, to a
'rationally' controlled urbanised society, and to what William
Bateson called 'the blighted atomistic individualism of the utili-
tarians'. (14) The interests of classes and occupations which
depended upon the traditional order, land rather than manufacture,
the country rather than the city, scriptural rather than scientistic authority, made for hostility to eugenics and its associated
lore and cosmology. Thus we have here a controversy sustained by
two sets of conflicting incompatible particular social interests,
associated with different sectors of the social structure. (15)

There is a sense in which it could be said that as situated, at

a particular time in a particular context, biometry was a form of
bourgeois-liberal thought and the Mendelism then opposed to it a
manifestation of conservative thought; but it is important to
remember the previously stated restrictions upon what such an imputation can be taken to imply. It says nothing about the intrinsic
characteristics of the knowledge involved. (16) Nor does it imply
that the knowledge, or the controversy itself, was bound to arise
given the state of society and culture in England at the time. Nor
does it predict individual attitudes and behaviour, or even necessarily, trends and tendencies in them.

It cannot be assumed that an individual with bourgeois origins,
or an occupation as a middle-class professional, would prefer the
biometrical account of inheritance and evolution to the Mendelian;
nor is it strictly justified to claim that there must be a tendency
for such an individual to have that preference. Individuals may
react against their backgrounds and the presuppositions of their
community of origin. Their occupational interests may be protected by institutional forms in which they have no involvement, using
knowledge claims and legitimations of whose content and function
they are ignorant. Such situations may be unusual, but the point
being made is not an empirical one. The point is that, formally,
the wrong level of analysis is involved here.

Basically, the implications of the imputation lie at the structural level. The central claim being made is that, in the absence
of the social-structural factors referred to, the controversy would
never have emerged, at least in the particular form observed. (17)
But of more empirical significance are two further implications,
both of which link the future development of the controversy to
changes in the social structure. First, one would expect the
controversy to decline in significance if social structural changes
weakened the particular interests sustaining it, or lessened the
effective conflict between those interests, or attenuated the effects
which such interests could have within the esoteric context of
'scientific' debate. (18) Second, one would expect major modifications of those claims or dogmas most strongly related to particular
interests, if social-structural changes resulted in their no longer
being the most expedient means of furthering or legitimating the
interests.

There is evidence to support both these expectations. As conservative interests have declined over the course of the century in
Britain, so too has their influence upon science generally, and
the study of inheritance in particular. (19) And at the same time
the development of instrumentally valuable competences from the
cultural resources of both Mendelism and biometry has circumvented
or incidentally eliminated many of the initial points of controversy between the two approaches. As far as the second expecta-
tion is concerned, it is interesting to note the remarkable decline
of eugenics in the years after 1918, and the associated redirection
of biometrical techniques away from evolutionary biology toward
formal statistical problems. MacKenzie (1976) suggests that this
decline occurred because conciliatory relationships with all
sections of the lower orders were the preferred ruling-class
strategy in post-war Britain, and offers of eugenic intervention
were accordingly unlikely to reap support and recognition for the

professional middle class. Before 1918 it had been possible to
attack the 'residuum', the destitute lower orders, without alienat-
ing the working class in general, which could be set up in contrast
as a valuable, indeed essential, part of the community. After the
war however, in conditions of greatly increased unemployment and
working-class militancy, the necessary accommodation with the workers
could not exclude an alleged 'residuum' of unemployed as a distinct,
separate group. Unemployment, it became apparent, was less a matter
of individual inadequacy, as the eugenists had implied, than of
fortune and social-structural factors. This changed perception was
itself the product of structural change, change which rendered
eugenics ideologically inexpedient and thus ensured its decline.

Great stress has been laid here upon the formal priority and the
empirical respectability of structural explanation, since this has
proved difficult to appreciate for those with predominantly individualistic patterns of thought. But the point must be counter-
balanced by recognising that the study of particular individuals,
their beliefs and their activity, is of paramount importance,
methodologically and empirically, in the sociology of knowledge. (20)
The existence of social structure, and of the public representations
and shared competences we call knowledge, becomes apparent to us
through the study of individuals, their utterances and their actions.
The properties of social structures are always manifested in particular concrete contexts via the behaviour of particular people. (21)

As it happens, most of the empirical material relevant to the
preceding example was obtained by biographical study of Karl Pearson,
William Bateson and a small group of related individuals. (22)
And Pearson and Bateson, in particular, can easily be taken as
typical representatives of two opposed social classes or categories.
Pearson, the son of a London lawyer and a Quaker family, educated at
University College school, was a typical radical middle-class intellectual who involved himself with appropriate political and social
causes from his early days at university: Darwinism, feminism
and rational-ethical alternatives to religion all quickly attracted
his interest, and, later, 'socialism' and social imperialism.
Bateson was the son of a solidly Anglican Cambridge academic; he
valued the Cambridge way of life and all that it symbolised, and
found the ever more intrusive consequences of industrialisation
distasteful. Less overtly political than Pearson, he nevertheless
can be clearly identified as a 'conservative thinker' and one who
consistently opposed the cause of radical reform. Both men clearly
set out in their own statements explicit links between their
political views and interests, and their scientific beliefs. (23)

When, as is so often the case in the sociology of knowledge, our
evidence is of this kind, arising out of the study of individual
biography, it can be hard to acknowledge that it is best taken as
support for structural hypotheses. Because the evidence concerns
individuals, it is tempting to think that it refers to the properties
of isolated individuals and is best explained in terms of other
properties of isolated individuals. It is tempting to 'explain' say
Pearson's scientific ideas by reference to his political ideas, his
background and previous experience, or his general social position,
as though these factors necessarily had determinate predictable
effects upon his thinking. And it is tempting to generalise such

explanation into hypotheses about what individuals with certain
characteristics must think, or are liable to think because of some
causal influence pressing upon their thought. Somehow, individual-
istically aligned explanation seems appropriate, economical and
scientific, particularly when the data to which it is addressed is
apparently 'about' individuals. But all this is a misconception.
Such 'explanations' can only possess plausibility if accompanied by
detailed assumptions about individual psychology, and about the
psychology of particular individuals, which we are in no position to
make.

We should rather take our data about individuals as evidence for
structural hypotheses in the way already discussed. There will, to
be sure, often be strong correlations between the backgrounds,
beliefs and current affiliations of the groups of individuals we
subject to empirical study. But there is little justification for
treating these as the cumulative consequences of the operation of
psychological cause-effect mechanisms. Indeed they can frequently
be related to structural factors on the basis of minimal psychological assumptions. Sociological theories give us no warrant for
assuming any necessary or determined links in the claims of affiliations, actions and utterances which make up individual biographies;
we should provisionally accept that different individuals in similar
contexts, with similar backgrounds, may fashion any number of such
chains. (24) But the links themselves must, for the most part, be
selected from given possibilities, the overall range of which will
be affected by social-structural factors. And in many societies it
happens that individuals moving into adult life from different
backgrounds encounter different ranges of sub-cultures and institutional forms with which they can affiliate. Since these initial
affiliations influence later opportunities for further affiliations,
typical overall ways of life and patterns of individual biography
emerge wherein various affiliations, activities and beliefs are
correlated. (25) Consequently, certain legitimations and forms of
knowledge do indeed tend predominantly to be held by certain speci-
fiable kinds of individual; but this is a consequence of the social
structure framing possible individual choices, and not of individuals
responding to some specific psychological constraint, or necessity.

The second concrete example to be discussed affords the maximum
possible contrast with that above, and provides some of the general
themes of this whole chapter with a valuable source of problems,
implicit criticisms and alternative formulations. In Lucien
Goldmann's splendid and endlessly fascinating 'The Hidden God'(1964)
an entire 'world-view', and not some particular features of instrumentally oriented knowledge, is imputed to a social class. And, so
far as one can judge without the historical competences relevant to
appraising the empirical material, the thesis and its justification
represents one of the finest examples of the sociological treatment
of knowledge and culture. (26) In what follows there is space to
go into only a very limited number of the findings and hypotheses
presented in the book.

The social basis of the material Goldmann studies he holds to lie
in the predicament of the 'noblesse de robe' in mid-seventeenth-
century France. This social class (27) had differentiated from the
Third Estate and developed separate rights and privileges over a

long period, supported by the king. In his long struggle to curb
the nobility the king had allied himself with the Third Estate and
drawn administrators and lawyers from their ranks into his service;
these came to constitute the 'noblesse de robe'. In the sixteenth
century they had considered themselves the main pillars of support
of the monarchy.

That support, however, had in a sense been too powerful. The
king had become so strong that he could aspire to absolutism, and
attempt to govern through administrators more directly his own
creatures than the semi-autonomous 'noblesse de robe'. Hence, his
policy changed to one of cautious hostility to the latter group,
whose rights he gradually squeezed and evaded, and whose institutions he patiently undermined. In the mid-seventeenth century this
process was well on the way to success and the king's aim was
practically ensured; the legal and administrative functions of the
'officiers' of the 'nobless de robe' were being diverted to 'com-
missaires' and 'Intendants', their 'Parlements' were losing power,
the value of their offices was ceasing to rise. (28)

This put the 'officiers' in what Goldmann calls a paradoxical
position. They were being attacked by the king and had good cause
to oppose him and work for his downfall. Yet such power and
privileges as they possessed depended entirely upon the existence
of the monarchy; to bring about its collapse would have been to
effect their own destruction. Their interests as a class appeared
to be incapable of being furthered by any practicable programme of
action.

Responses to this situation followed a number of patterns. The
majority of 'officiers' accommodated themselves to the increased
power of the king, and in many cases oriented their ambitions to
offices directly under his control; they sought functions in the
bureaucracy which was undermining their current position and oppos-
ing their colleagues and their overall community. Others went into
direct opposition, allied themselves with anti-monarchist elements
in the Third Estate, and consequently, according to Goldmann, took
up the 'bourgeois' ideology of rationalism. A few practised withdrawal and refusal of the world, and gained thereby widespread
sympathy and support from others; they sold their offices to
become 'solitaires' and justified themselves by an ideology of
withdrawal - Jansenism, the subject of Goldmann's analysis.

Jansenism between 1640 and 1670, as studied by Goldmann, included
a number of texts and doctrines, often conflicting the one with the
other. At one pole it differed little formally from Calvinism, and
discoursed upon the problems of the good man seeking to endure, and
serve God, in a fundamentally evil world; it incorporated the
familiar apparatus of the elect and predestination. But more characteristically it stressed the irremediably evil state of the world
and the corrupt state of fallen man, in advocacy of the rejection
of worldly matters, withdrawal and silence. Always, in whatever
variant, it turned its face away from the world, toward God; and
always that God was as distant and remote as the God of Descartes,
whom bourgeois minds were content to set at the edge of things whilst
they turned to worldly matters. Jansenists and Cartesians conceptualised the existent world in much the same way; their
essential difference lay in how they evaluated it (cf. p. 8).

Goldmann advances the hypothesis that Jansenism was an ideology
of the 'noblesse de robe', and that its doctrines were determined
by the particular social interests of the 'officiers'. (29)   Moreover, the manner in which he substantiates and justifies this
imputation is admirable in practically every way.   He always remains aware that the beliefs and interests with which he is dealing
are socially and culturally situated in a way which must be taken
into account in understanding the link between them. (30)   He
attempts, in so far as it is possible, to ascertain who actively
advocated the Jansenist doctrines and who opposed them, who were
sympathetic to the cause and who were not.   He cites individual
cases of men selling their legal offices and becoming 'solitaires'.
But, despite this respect for empirical evidence and the concrete
examination of historical materials, Goldmann is never in the
slightest danger of interpreting his materials in an individualistic
perspective.   He does not seek to rest his case upon the percentage
of 'officiers' who were sympathetic to Jansenism, or the percentage
of Jansenist sympathisers who were 'officiers', or any other
measure of the frequency of belief within a population of
individuals.

Goldmann's is explicitly a structural hypothesis, informed by his
overall view of the structure of seventeenth-century French society.
Biographical materials and statistics about groups of individuals
are treated as evidence of the contingent routes via which particular interests achieved expression;   they are given significance
in the light of general knowledge of the social structure. (31)
Nor are they by any means the only kinds of evidence to which
Goldmann appeals.   He discusses the correlation of the ideology
of withdrawal with social structural changes in France, and attempts
to show that it only attained any real importance when his own
favoured causal factor was a prominent structural feature. (32)
And (perhaps most significantly of all to his own mind) he examines
the internal, conceptual characteristics of the Jansenist doctrines,
and demonstrates in detail the ways in which they can be taken as
expressions of the predicament of the 'officiers', legitimations
of their policies, and adjuncts of their interests.   On the basis
of this examination he is prepared to argue that the only really
consistent Jansenists were the Blaise Pascal of the 'Pensées' and
the Jean Racine of 'Phèdre' and the other tragedies;   neither were
by any stretch of the imagination typical representatives of the
'noblesse de robe', and the latter, by his involvement with the
theatre, had set himself in explicit opposition to the Jansenist
hierarchy. (33)

Inevitably, however, there are important points of divergence
between Goldmann's version of dialectical materialism, much influenced by the thought of Georg Lukács, and the naturalistic
position taken in this book.   Many of these are well illustrated
by his treatment of the works of Pascal and Racine, wherein he
discerns a unique tragic and paradoxical expression of the Jansénist
doctrines.   These exceptional individuals, he suggests, constructed
a world vision embodying in a peculiarly coherent and perfect form
the situation and objectives of the 'noblesse de robe'.   This was a
vision only partially and imperfectly realised in the thought of
less sensitive men, even if they were more typical representatives

of the class in question. Pascal and Racine embodied in their work
the most advanced form of consciousness possible to the 'noblesse de
robe'; their thought was closest to the essence of the thought of
the class, to what should be properly imputed to it as its consciousness; in a sense they were the only real Jansenists (p. 18).

This claim is justified by three kinds of argument. First,
Goldmann attempts to show by textual analysis that Pascal, in particular, developed the logical implications of Jansenism more ex-
tensively and systematically than anyone else, and that his thought
was less diverted by expedient considerations and the practical
exigencies of the moment than was that of other writers. It would
be easy to make superficial criticisms of this argument by pointing
to the contradictions and formal inconsistencies which Goldmann himself stresses in his discussion of Pascal's 'Pensées', but this
would be to miss his point. (34) There is indeed a sense in which
these writings, long matured by someone not distracted by the
perpetual crises of the fully involved political life, might be said
to go further and exhibit greater coherence than the thoughts of
others. Even so, this would not justify the claim that Pascal had
developed a particular form of consciousness as far as it was capable of going.

Goldmann's second form of justification is essentially dogmatic.
He sets Pascal's tragic vision upon a line of historical progress
from bourgeois rationalism to dialectical materialism, as a transitional form of consciousness associated with a transitional social
form or class. (35) And he simply asserts that the transition from
tragic vision to genuine dialectics was impossible without social
change. Pascal had generated a more advanced form of consciousness
than his contemporaries, as evidenced by its closer approach than
theirs to the perspective of dialectical materialism, but the social
determinants of his thought in his particular context precluded
further advance. The next stage of historical progress had to occur
first in the material sphere and not in the realm of ideas.

It is here that Goldmann approaches most closely to Georg Lukacs,
both in terminology and style of explanation. The above argument is,
of course, a teleological one and cannot be accepted by anyone with
a naturalistic perspective. It assumes that history has a meaning,
that a pathway is, as it were, set out in front of it or that some
force or power is pulling it forward. There is no point in considering the relative merits of naturalistic and teleological
assumptions here. But it is worth noting that Goldmann, unlike
others who employ them, (36) is well aware of the teleological presuppositions in his thought, and explicitly acknowledges their
existence. Indeed, he provides a studied defence of them (chapter
5), which is worth attention as one of the very few coherent justifications of such a standpoint.

Goldmann's third argument is the most important and interesting.
It is that Pascal and Racine exhibit in their literary productions
'the maximum possible awareness of the social group whose nature
they are expressing' (p. 17). Most of 'The Hidden God' is devoted
to a detailed analysis of the work of Pascal and Racine, in order
to demonstrate the extent of this awareness. The form of the
analysis is, however, by no means a typical dialectical materialist
treatment of ideas. In the context of his detailed textual com-

mentary, the real interests of the 'noblesse de robe' tend to be forgotten; their aims, aspirations and political strategies fade from prominence; even the social functions of their beliefs as rationalisations and legitimations are given only a secondary emphasis. What is given priority is an exploration of formal analogies between the structure of ideas and the real social structure in which the 'officiers' were located. The work of Pascal and Racine exhibits the maximum awareness of the conditions of the 'noblesse de robe' because its structures make the most perfect and developed analogy with the real structure of social life of the 'officiers' as a class; of all Jansenist literature its underlying organisation is the most nearly isomorphous with the social structure.

It would be pointless to attempt to summarise Goldmann's exposition and substantiation of this hypothesis, since it involves a great range of textual interpretations and comparisons extending over many pages and achieving their effect cumulatively. Its general import can, however, be conveyed if some risk of parody is accepted. (37) When a class or community is under external threat or pressure it typically turns in upon its own resources for sustenance. The ideological analogue of this in religious idiom is a rejection of the world in favour of God. If there is hope of triumphing over or containing the opposition, then the world may be condemned as the evil environment in which to fight for goodness and justice. If a group has little power but a strong communal bond and little dependence on the favour of others, it may develop a mystical religion where the world is rejected in favour of a close, intimate relationship with God; the immediate relationship with God is the analogue of the close communal relationships within the threatened group. Generally, the rejection of wordly values and concerns is the analogue of oppositon to the social order and the pressure of its institutions; the proximity of God is the analogue of the presence of community and the strength of the affective links it provides.

When we turn to the 'officiers' we find a class who were indeed under structural pressure, and who might be expected to have set their face against the world. They were, moreover, a class with some considerable power, which could be turned against the existing order of things. But here they were in an intolerable dilemma, since the power they possessed was the product of the existing order, and derived from the very institutional forms which were putting them under pressure. When they set themselves against the world, their communal strengths could avail them nothing; to undermine oppressing institutions would have been to undermine their own existence. Hence when they turned away from the world it was to a God distant and obscure; the God whom they knew to exist, of whom they were directly aware, as they are aware of their communal life, was also a hidden God who could not help them. Thus, their God was properly the God of the extreme Jansenists, distant and unresponsive, a source of moral judgment but not material assistance. And their proper doctrine was one which demanded rejection of an evil world, yet offered no hope of changing it, and hence condemned dialogue or interaction with it as pointless and absurd; the good life involved withdrawal from all worldly matters and solitary dialogue with God.

This is the doctrinal position which Goldmann associates with the writings of Martin de Barcos. It is a less perfect analogue of social reality than the works of Pascal and Racine only because it does not stress the *paradoxical* aspects of the situation of the 'officiers':

> . . . their legal functions made them economically dependent, as *officiers,* upon a monarchical state whose growth they opposed from an ideological and political point of view. This put them in an eminently paradoxical situation - and one which, in my view, provides the infrastructure for the tragic paradox of *Phèdre* and of the *Pensées* - where they were strongly opposed to a form of government which they could not try to destroy or even to alter in any radical manner. (p. 120)

The 'Pensées', according to Goldmann, develop Jansenism to the point of paradox, paradox which they expose and celebrate as an essential feature of their own structure. At the same time, they reveal all meaningful human activity to be itself grounded in paradox. For Pascal, the absence of God from the world, his exile beyond the infinite reaches of empty space, means that his existence can no longer be proved. Despite the felt certainty of his presence, one must wager upon his very existence; he is both absent and present at the same time. Analogously, since God is absent and hidden, and never makes response to those who turn to him, there is no way to turn from the world. The world must both be rejected and accepted at the same time; it is without value but is to be lived in. As for those good men who seek God, there is no guarantee that he will be found; implicit in the cosmology of the 'Pensées' is the final paradox of the existence of the righteous sinner, of the sincere prayer which is not granted. (38)

Hence Goldmann takes the 'Pensées' as offering the most perfect structural analogue of the predicament of the 'noblesse de robe', the most profound philosophical representation of their social situation. And, with the proviso that the empirical base of his hypotheses may eventually prove inadequate, it is easy to accept the main thrust of his argument. What is less acceptable from a naturalistic perspective is the use of the analysis to support the view that Pascal's thought was the most 'advanced' form of Jansenism, and that it represented the most advanced form of consciousness possible at the time. A naturalistic account must be content to take Goldmann as demonstrating the particularly far-reaching influence of social perception and experience in the development of a philosophical work. (39)

In many ways indeed this structural analysis of Goldmann's is analogous to the later work of Emile Durkheim. Durkheim, in 'De Quelques Formes primitives de classification' (1903), and 'Les Formes elementaires de la vie religieuse' (1912), attempted to show that cosmologies and natural classifications were modelled on the analogy of the classifications of society. (40) And at several points he at least hinted at the idea that direct unverbalised social experience could act as a model, by analogy with which classifications and verbally organised structures could be created. (41) This is very much the form of explanation implied in the textual commentaries of 'The Hidden God'. It is true that

the latter, with its sensitivity to the role of interest in the
generation of culture, and its understanding of conflict as organised
around social-structural cleavages, provides a more satisfactory
model for the sociology of knowledge than does Durkheim's work.
But given that Goldmann does not adequately integrate his accounts
of Jansenism as strategic ideology and Jansenism as the self-
awareness of a class, and given his reliance upon unsatisfactory
forms of teleological explanation, there is much to be said for
using both bodies of writing as resources in understanding and dealing with the difficulties of the other. (42)

Chapter 4

THE PROBLEM OF THE
POWER OF KNOWLEDGE AND IDEAS

1 HISTORICAL MATERIALISM

The problem of the power of knowledge and ideas and particularly of
their significance in the understanding of social change has always
been an important and controversial issue, polarising historians
and sociologists between various kinds of idealism on the one hand
and materialism on the other. In practice, idealists have tended
to understand history in terms of the general principles and ideas
which men profess, and are presumed to possess; they have assumed
that action is inferred from and hence determined by such general
principles. Historical materialism, in reaction to this, has
given primacy to social activity itself and the given forms in which
it exists.

In the 'German Ideology' (1970), Marx and Engels produced a first
informal sketch of what has become known as historical materialism.
History was not a progression of disembodied ideas, but an ongoing
process actively generated by men, producing their means of sub-
sistence in co-operative interaction with others. In the course of
productive activity men acted upon and changed the natural world;
and thereby they changed themselves, their social relationships and
patterns of organisation, and their consciousness. Hence men were
not the puppets of ideas; rather, through their own concrete
activity, knowingly or unknowingly, they made their own history.

Empirical observation must in each separate instance bring out
empirically, and without any mystification and speculation, the
connection of the social and political structure with production.
The social structure and the State are continually evolving out
of the life-process of definite individuals, but of individuals,
not as they may appear in their own or other people's imagination, but as they *really* are; i.e. as they operate, produce
materially, and hence as they work under definite material limits,
presuppositions and conditions independent of their will. . . .

In direct contrast to German philosophy which descends from
heaven to earth, here we ascend from earth to heaven. . . .
We set out from real active men, and on the basis of their real
life-process we demonstrate the development of the ideological
reflexes and echoes of this life-process. (1970, p. 47)

There is no doubt of the value of this broad conception. It
has inspired outstanding historical studies, notably those of Marx
himself; and it has usefully extended the perception even of
scholars who have chosen to excoriate the materialist standpoint.
Yet it has proved extraordinarily difficult to develop into a
systematic account of the process of social change, and of the role
of knowledge and ideas therein. (1) Certainly, the many attempts
to transform historical materialism into a 'scientific' theory of
history, which accounts for social change independently of these
factors, have merely demonstrated the futility of such an enterprise.

Such attempts constitute an important strand of materialist
thought, presumably because they imply that materialist analysis can
claim certainty for its predictions, and that the success of
revolutionary socialism can be shown to be inevitable. Typically,
they insist that the course of social change can be predicted from
objective laws, that it is determined by the operation of some
particular objective factor (hence the tendency for historical materialism to be equated with economic determinism, or technological
determinism or historicism). They treat consciousness, conceived
as including knowledge and ideas, as entirely derivative. If this
were not done - if it were admitted that knowledge could be an
autonomous determining factor in social change - then that which we
did not yet know could, on becoming known, influence the future.
Certainly as to the outcome of social change would entail omni-
science. Hence, ideas and knowledge of all kinds are designated
as superstructural and placed in a strictly derivative relationship
to the economic base or foundation of society. The base, con-
stituting the forces and relations of production, is treated as a
sufficient cause of the superstructure. And similarly within the
base itself, the relations of production, being social conventions
and hence distressingly subjective phenomena, are made strictly
derivative of the forces of production. Objective factors like
productive forces, technique and technology, are all that remain to
drive the motor of history.

Needless to say, there are no grounds whatsoever for according
credibility to this scientistic form of materialism. It is worth
brief mention only in order to note the manner in which its terminology glosses over the historical significance of knowledge and ideas.
Without necessarily objecting to their use in explanation, we are
entitled to ask for the referents of such terms as 'productive
forces', 'technique' or 'technology'. We cannot, for example,
identify productive forces simply as sets of physical objects lying
around in the environment of a society; nor can we say that the
nature of a productive resource as an object inherently determines
its employment or use.

Neither the crude raw materials used in production, nor the
objective character of the given tools of production, can be held
to determine production itself. They are raw materials and tools
only because they are conceptualised and operated upon in a certain
way, only because, that is, of the meaning imputed to them and the
knowledge of them which people possess. Production is necessarily
the accomplishment of cognitively competent, knowledgeable, social-
ised groups of men. The productive forces of a society must be considered as institutions. And the activities of producing

individuals, like any institutionalised activities must be understood as inextricably incorporating their knowledge: knowledge of
the social relationships they are involved in, knowledge embedded
in their productive competences and skills, knowledge of these
competences such as makes possible their future refinement and
development. We must not imagine that production, or any kind of
institutionalised activity, can be analysed into independent
components of belief and behaviour, so that the latter can be held
to determine the former. One consequence of this is that it
becomes impossible to explain why behaviour should ever change.
Rather, we must recognise that social change has to be understood
as, and in terms of, meaningful behaviour, that is, behaviour
suffused with knowledge, or, as we are able unambiguously to say
today, activity. With our current conception of activity, simply
to use the term in the explanation of social change is tantamount
to acknowledging the real significance of knowledge in history.

It seems clear that no account of social change is acceptable
which denies the role of the knowledge and the competences which
people collectively sustain and transmit. Accounts which apparently
ignore them, if they present any appearance of plausibility at all,
are likely to involve indirect, covert references to them, as was
the case with the scientistic materialism mentioned above. We
cannot sift knowledge, ideas, concepts and all else that smacks
of consciousness, out of history, and find remaining some hard,
objective referents, which can be cited as the real causes of
social change. According to the sieve we use we find all of
history passing through, or none.

Emphatically, however, this conclusion should not be taken as an
argument for even a partial reversion to an idealist position. Nor
does it imply that all the components of a society and its culture
should be given equal consideration in the study of social change.
Idealism, as it has come to be understood by sociologists in the
context of this debate, is every bit as unsatisfactory a position
as scientistic materialism.

2 WEBER

Perhaps the most celebrated idealist response to historical
materialism is Max Weber's study of 'The Protestant Ethic and the
Spirit of Capitalism' (1930), the argument of which is sufficiently
well known to require no detailed exposition here. Strictly
speaking, Weber's thesis is not idealist, but eclectic. It does
not assert the priority of ideas in history but merely claims that
ideas, as much as material factors, may operate as significant
historical causes. No single kind of factor is to be given priority
in social change; everything may causally interact with everything
else. Such eclecticism wins ready praise from many sociologists,
who see it as an undogmatic and moderate position reasonably well
supported by Weber's extensive historical work. Yet it is surely
suspect. Weber's eclectism simply runs incompatible idealist and
materialist forms of explanation in parallel, without any attempt
at synthesis or the resolution of contradiction. And, with two
theories to choose from at any particular time rather than one, it

is not surprising that the results of his laborious but basically
uninformative comparative historical studies always prove
compatible with his schemes of 'explanation'.

Thus, in examining Weber's ideas as alternatives to historical
materialism it is only necessary to consider their idealist component. This can always be plucked, whole and undigested, from
the total context of his argument, leaving a residue more or less
compatible with the materialist view of history. In the particular
case of the Weber thesis itself, such an approach produces considerable economy of effort. We can set on one side the many quali-
fications and auxiliary hypotheses with which Weber surrounded his
central idealist claim and concentrate entirely upon the positive
significance of the claim itself. As we shall see, the arguments
in its favour are quite extraordinarily thin for a thesis so
celebrated and widely accepted. And there are in Weber's own text
many pieces of evidence and potential inferences which count
directly against it. (2)

Weber held that a particular set of ideas or beliefs were shown
by his work to have been essential in the production of an important social change. The ideas were those of ascetic protestantism, and Calvinism in particular. The social change was the rise
of modern rational capitalism. Weber claimed that the moral maxims
and cosmological theories of Calvinism predated the rise of capitalism, and were a necessary cause of that rise; that is, in the
absence of those maxims and theories, modern capitalism would not
have been able to follow the particular course of development via
which it actually became a dominant set of institutional forms. (3)

That such an hypothesis stands opposed to historical materialism
is obvious enough; but the extent to which it challenges the latter
perspective is worth emphasising. The social change in question,
the rise of modern capitalism, is precisely the subject of Marx's
main historical work 'Capital'. The ideas in question, the moral
maxims of Calvinism, are of the most general and abstract kind,
and are, moreover, situated in the context of religion, far removed
from the activity of production; such ideas could scarcely be
treated as essential determinants of social change from the standpoint of historical materialism. This stark contrast makes the
thesis of the 'Protestant Ethic' a particularly appropriate example
with which to assess Weber's idealism. Yet it is by no means an
extreme expression of his views; general ideas, maxims and values
continue to be treated as major determinants throughout his later
detailed cross-cultural studies.

In order to evaluate the thesis in general terms, let us
temporarily accept all of Weber's empirical claims: that ascetic
protestantism did predate rational capitalism, that there was a
clear association of the two phenomena, and so on. And let us also
acquiesce in the general features of Weber's method, such as his
construction of 'ideal types'. This will allow us to concentrate
upon two particularly important theoretical questions.

First, if Calvinism was not 'the ideology of capitalism', but an
independent phenomenon, we are entitled to ask what gave rise to
that phenomenon. Such a question is surely more puzzling than the
equivalent problem of understanding how a new 'material factor'
arises in society. Historical materialism is intuitively plausible

in social-psychological terms; it seems reasonable that new methods of production and modes of economic organisation should arise as communities seek to further their interests and satisfy their needs in their particular given social situations. But the maxims and cosmology of Calvinism are altogether more problematic. We surely cannot believe that they naturally arose in the rational progress of theology. Nor should we evade the problem by dipping selected Reformation divines in hypothetical vats of 'charisma'. Presumably, ascetic protestantism must be seen as the product of some earlier constellation of factors, not including capitalism. Its character-istic ideas must have been developed in response to some earlier situation, and must subsequently have had unintended consequences for the actors who developed and accepted them; the ideas must have determined activities in unanticipated ways. Such a position does indeed seem reasonably to represent Weber's own view. He did not claim that Calvinist ideas were themselves undetermined, but merely that they were a link in an ongoing causal chain of equivalent importance to any other link.

This, however, immediately raises a general difficulty with Weber's eclectic position. His main thesis is best sustained if the Calvinist maxims are regarded as having been strong deter-minants of action, and if a general claim is made to the effect that men are strongly determined by the general principles and beliefs to which they hold. But the more strongly actors are held to be determined by their ideas and beliefs, the more puzzling does conceptual innovation and cultural change become. The people who set aside their previous ideas to invent or accept Calvinist doctrine are among those whose behaviour becomes more difficult to understand. Clearly, without some theory which reconciles the potency of Calvin's maxims as determinants of action with their status as the inventions and tools of men, Weber's explanations stand as no more than empty rationalisations; men are determined by their beliefs except when they are not. For the most part, Weber overlooked the need for a theory of this kind; just occasionally, however, he does barely hint at one way of resolving the difficulty. In a number of places where he discusses modifications of doctrine one is led to wonder whether Weber did not regard élites and intel-lectuals as in control of ideas, and ideas as in control of ordinary men (cf. 1930, pp. 110-12). The notion that some kinds of men are determined by ideas and other kinds are not would at least rescue Weber's overall explanatory scheme from complete vacuity.

This leads us on to the second question, that of the way in which the Calvinist maxims caused the changes in activity which eventually gave rise to rational capitalism. Two possible modes of deter-mination are commonly considered here, logical and psychological; and it is generally accepted that Weber himself stressed the latter. Indeed, one is almost bound to accept this if one places any credi-bility in Weber's thesis, since his empirical materials are so immediately unfavourable to the former possibility. If we accept Weber's account of the maxims themselves, and we draw what seem to be the obvious logical conclusions from them, (4) we arrive at a number of enjoined forms of activity, some of which would evi-dently favour the rise of capitalism, and some of which clearly would not. If we take the favourable implications (hard work, an ascetic mode of life, etc.) to support the logical variant of Weber's thesis, then the equally numerous and significant unfavourable implications (irrelevance of worldly activity, submission to clerical authority, abolition of usury, etc.) must be held to count against it. The original Calvinist maxims evidently legiti- mate appropriate capital generating activity no more successfully than would randomly selected aphorisms. Nor is it at all helpful to point out that some of the least appropriate maxims were amended by Calvin's followers. This returns us to the dilemma previously discussed: the vacuity of the thesis that ideas deter- mine action or else they do not remain in the claim that logic determines people's conclusions save when they decide to change their premises.

Unfortunately, the psychological variant of Weber's thesis is in no way preferable. According to this account, the Calvinist cos- mology, in which the fate of all individuals had been irrevocably and unknowably decided by God, was psychologically intolerable. Not to have any hope of objective knowledge of who was of the elect and who of the damned was too much to be borne. Despite the ex- plicit tenet of their faith that salvation could not be assured by works or any worldly activity, men found themselves looking to such things as signs of their election. Wealth and worldly success became valued as sources of reassurance for the faithful, and this even gained recognition at the level of doctrine as Calvinism evolved (or, perhaps better, degenerated). Hence, there was an intense concern with the acquisition of wealth, on the part of indi- viduals whose ascetic moral code permitted them no legitimate means of dissipating it through consumption. And the consequent tendency to capital accumulation eventually created the conditions for the transition to modern rational capitalism. As the accidental consequence of their cleavage to their faith, the Calvinists and related communities brought into existence a way of life which would have appalled anyone who cherished its maxims.

The extent of the credibility which has been accorded to this feeble rationalisation is quite extraordinary. Evidently, we are invited to believe that the doctrine of predestination failed to determine people's actions because they found it psychologically intolerable, whereas the injunction to asceticism, presumably being less psychologically offensive, did so determine them. Perhaps some profound but unstated psychological principles are being assumed here, which would vindicate the above claim, and explain how the Calvinists might have developed an acquisitive way of life in order to provide themselves with a form of personal reassurance which their faith insisted was no such thing. But, more likely, we are simply in the realm of fantasy. As far as the empirical materials of Weber's book are a valid indication, the complete converse of the above would indeed appear to be more probable. Arguably, Calvin's original doctrine of predestination, its initial functions having become less significant, was corrupted through the desire of the faithful to account what they were *already* doing as being of cosmological significance. The wealth they were busily acquiring was given a religious rationale as a sign of election.

Interpretations of this kind are never given detailed con- sideration by Weber, even as subsidiary themes to his main hypothesis. Ideas are the protagonists of his extraordinarily overrated work. Singly and in constellations they appear as 'dramatis personae' in the pages of the 'Protestant Ethic', pulling the strings of puppets to generate required historical sequences. That this theatrical re-enactment requires great efforts of stage management to achieve any semblance of illusion should not surprise us. Rather it should suggest that at the original performance it was the puppets who pulled the strings, and that the reified ideas of the dramatist's imagination derived from the continually adapted justifications of changing ways of life.

There is one difficulty, and only one, which Weber's study sets in the way of analyses of this kind, and which must be dealt with if Calvinist doctrine is to be treated as derivative, and not as an inceptive, consequential historical phenomenon. This is the empirical claim that the Calvinist maxims preceded, by a considerable margin, the acquisitive, wealth-generating activities which led on to modern capitalism. If this was indeed the case then the original maxims could not have arisen as rationalisations of those same activities; and the apparent link between maxims and activities must have been the consequence of a causal link from the former to the latter as Weber maintained, or of a link through a third factor, or of chance. Here are a series of problems which will have to be settled gradually as more and more concrete historical studies accumulate. But it is worth noting in the present context the fascinating and far-reaching implications of one of the most recent empirical reassessments of the Weber thesis, that of H. R. Trevor-Roper. His conclusions in 'Religion, the Reformation and Social Change' (1967), for all that they represent the views of a notably conservative historian, are far easier to reconcile with a broadly materialist position than with Weber's brand of idealism.

The association of Calvinism and capitalism was, according to Trevor-Roper's evidence, essentially the product of a third factor. The really significant cause of the rise of rational capitalism in northern Europe was *immigration*. Elements of the long-established financial élites of southern Europe, moving north under pressure from the counter-Reformation, applied their traditional skills in a new context of opportunities. They used their techniques for systematic control and organisation in new contexts of trade, and eventually of manufacture. In societies where the state could not call upon the vast court bureaucracies of the catholic south, and hence could not so successfully restrict and exploit their industry, they were peculiarly successful. Their comparatively unrestrained activities succeeded in shifting the balance of economic power to protestant northern Europe, and this in itself explains many of the associations of protestantism and capitalism to which Weber drew attention.

Although the religious beliefs of the important groups of migrant entrepreneurs were by no means uniform, a considerable proportion of them possessed what Trevor-Roper describes as 'Erasmian' views. They had traditionally held to the humanistic, anti-clerical, anti-ritualistic varieties of catholicism characteristic of the secular élites of Italy and other catholic states. When the schisms of the Reformation and the attendant

political and military pressures put these societies under threat,
power swung to the church, and social control was intensified.
Catholic dogma was more narrowly and rigorously defined, so that
many of 'Erasmian' persuasion eventually found themselves, for the
first time, committed to heresy or something dangerously close to
it, simply by virtue of believing what they had always tended to
believe. At the same time, they were faced with increased tax-
ation, for military expansion and the increased splendour of court
and church adopted in the cause of social control. And despite
their material contributions to society, they found themselves
more and more in the position of a suspect and unvalued minority,
an enclave amidst an incompatible way of life. Hence an Erasmian
diaspora to the north.

Erasmianism is still far removed from ascetic Calvinism. But
so too, according to Trevor-Roper, were the main entrepreneurial
groups involved in the rise of capitalism. Trevor-Roper devotes
much of his paper to demonstrating that the way of life, even of
the Calvinist entrepreneurs, was anything but ascetic. And many
of the entrepreneurs were not Calvinists at all, but expressed
their Erasmianism in protestant form as Arminianism or Anglican-
ism. They were intimately associated with authentic Calvinist
communities by force of circumstances. External pressure from
Catholic powers and the agents of the counter-Reformation was
always strong. Calvinist clerics with their demanding requirements
of their flocks, could organise populations to resist coercion.
And the alliance of the moderate protestantism of the capitalist
élites with the broader base of Calvinism was indeed most marked
at times of crisis and external military threat. Where Calvinism
enjoyed complete predominance in a society, on the other hand,
developments toward rational capitalism were arguably less in
evidence even than in Catholic countries: such was the state of
affairs, for example, in Scotland and the Palatinate.

What then are the general implications of Trevor-Roper's
brilliant reappraisal? First, and perhaps most important for
present purposes, the key element in Weber's empirical case is
refuted. Rational capitalism did not clearly post-date Calvinism;
it existed, albeit in a variant form, in catholic Europe, and
appeared as a transplant later in the north. The importance of
this point needs great stress. In an uncharacteristically in-
sensitive assessment of Trevor-Roper's views, Tom Burns has written
(1969, p. 12):

> Trevor-Roper's own suggestions, which substitute Erasmus for
> Calvin, migrant financiers for entrepreneurs, and the sixteenth
> century for the seventeenth, seem to me to do little more than
> shift the problem one stage further back without changing the
> general terms of the thesis he challenges.

In fact, the whole basis of Weber's attack upon materialism is
undermined by this change. No longer do we find beliefs in
existence before the activities which, allegedly, they eventually
determine. Instead, we find ideas co-existent with a recognisably
congruent way of life; ideas and activities here may plausibly
be held to have developed as one. Erasmianism is well characterised
as the religion and ideology of secular élites in the context of
Catholic Europe: it exalts lay activity; it seeks to restrain

clerical pretensions; it opposes institutional religion with private devotion; it encourages direct familiarity with the biblical texts. How clearly it expresses the rivalry between secular élites and those wielding the power of the institutions of the Church. A broadly materialist position faces few problems with a situation of this kind; there is nothing here which can be set up, for example, as a challenge to the analysis of the 'German Ideology':

> Men are the producers of their conceptions, ideas, etc. - real, active men . . .
>
> Morality, religion, metaphysics, all the rest of ideology and their corresponding forms of consciousness, thus no longer retain the semblance of independence. They have no history, no development; but men, developing their material production and their material intercourse, alter, along with this their real existence, their thinking and the products of their thinking. Life is not determined by consciousness, but consciousness by life. (Marx and Engels, 1970, p. 47)

We may reasonably take the religious maxims and doctrines of the early capitalist élites as expressing features of their concrete way of life, and reflecting practical problems of economic and political interaction. As these features and problems changed, before, during and after their diaspora, so too, as Trevor-Roper shows us, did their doctrines, which varied according to the degree of pressure they were under, and according to the alliances they were able to make. One does indeed find evidence of the same kind of variation in Weber's own work; but it is never stressed, since it fits so ill with his idealist argument. The pragmatic flexibility of doctrinal development, and indeed the straight expediency which many individuals revealed in their religious orientation, is more forthrightly described and realistically appraised by Trevor-Roper. One finds no particular concern to devalue the historical role of ideas in the work of this conservative writer; but this only makes the more compelling his refutation of Weber's idealism. To accept Trevor-Roper's evidence and interpretation is effectively to admit that a determining historical role for general principles and religious doctrines cannot be established by reference to the 'Protestant Ethic'.

We should not, however, be content to use Trevor-Roper simply as a means of undermining the Weber thesis. His own explanatory account deserves attention in its own right; as what is arguably the most coherent and best substantiated theory of the rise of modern capitalism, it has implications of great interest. Note that although general ideas and maxims depart from the centre of the stage, social change is still explained by reference to the distribution of knowledge and ideas. Esoteric knowledge, carried by a migrating population and transplanted into a new context, is the central explanatory factor in Trevor-Roper's account. But the knowledge involved is not of doctrines and aphorisms; it is techniques and competences. And new forms of activity arise not because men are determined by new ideas, but because they actively deploy their knowledge in a new context, as a resource to further their interests. Indeed, it is debatable whether to refer to the carriers of practical technical knowledge as the possessors of

ideas is not pointless and needlessly confusing. There is a world
of difference between theories which ascribe knowledge of this
kind an autonomous role in social change, and traditional idealist
theories in sociology, with their stress on the determining role
of values and maxims of conduct.

This point will be taken up again in the next section, but
before moving on to it there is yet another important feature of
Trevor-Roper's work to be examined. This is its fine sensitivity
to the social basis of Calvinism. Following Weber, most sociologists have characterised this as a particularly 'rational' form
of religion appropriate to individualistic, calculating,
'bourgeois' cultures. But this characterisation is, at best, a
partial one, and may indeed miss the most salient element of the
phenomenon. In seeking to understand Calvinism we must accept
that, as Weber insistently pointed out, 'the doctrine of predestination was considered its most characteristic dogma' (p. 98).
Weber correlated Calvin's divergence from Luther on this matter
with the former's greater logical consistency, and attempted to
present predestination as an extreme reaction to magical beliefs,
which imply the possibility of ritual intervention in the matter
of grace and salvation. But he might also have reflected upon the
way that the doctrine debars us from further knowledge of God's
decrees. 'Everything else, including the meaning of our individual
destiny, is hidden in dark mystery which it would be both impossible to pierce and presumptious to question' (p. 103).

At the level of doctrine, authentic Calvinism could well be
classed as a mystical and irrationalist faith. The object of its
worship is unknowable, publicly inaccessible, beyond the influence
of men and their institutions. The knowledge on which the believer
must rely derives from within his own individual psyche, in a
fashion unamenable to verbal description and inaccessible to external assistance or impediment. Following Mary Douglas (1970), we
expect such a religion to be that of a group at odds with dominant
institutions, and actively resisting threats from external
powers. (5) Such indeed was the predicament of the Calvinist International at the relevant point in time.

It is easy to miss the mystical irrationality of Calvinism for
two reasons. First, we associate such qualities with informal warm-
hearted sects and their cuddly cosmologies; the mystical doctrines
of our experience are held by soulful folk who pick flowers, love
each other and meditate. We are unprepared for austere, ascetic,
varieties of mysticism. Second, we observe the manifest efficiency
in the organisation of Calvinist society, and are struck by its
intense concrete involvement in worldly activity, its sheer
practical competence, its systematic mobilisation of resources.
These are the very virtues we attribute to our modern 'rational'
societies. Yet they served the same interest of protecting against
external threat as generated the doctrinal mysticism with which
they were combined.

With what we can admire as impeccable sociological intuition,
Trevor-Roper perceives this key aspect of the Calvinist doctrine
and way of life. Hence he is able convincingly to explain its rise,
its association with the rise of capitalism, its metamorphosis,
and its eventual decline. Calvinism, as an expression and

rationalisation of resistance to threat was bound to wane as the communities which sustained it met with success, secured themselves against enemies, and stabilised. For a time, however, such communities in Reformation Europe nurtured or gave protection to emerging forms of capitalist organisation, and enabled them to survive a critical period in their growth and institutionalisation.

Emphatically, however, not even an explanation of the rise and decline of a phenomenon like Calvinism can base itself simply upon references to social factors, and take no account of Knowledge and its social distribution. The pressures of the church and the various powerful state apparatus do not suffice to explain the growth of Calvinism. To see this, it is only necessary to remind ourselves of the existence of another movement reacting to these same pressures, that of the Anabaptists or Chiliasts, which was particularly strong among peasants and the lower layers of artisans. Here reaction against the pressure of dominant institutions took on a much more recognisably mystical form, with a close, unmediated, accessible God, a high valuation of warmth, fellowship and informality, and a general distrust of institutions and organisation.

Mannheim (1936) characterised Chiliasm as the Utopia of peasantry and lower orders, and had it correspond to their social position just as he held liberal humanism to be characteristically bourgeois. Yet the phenomenon represented a glaring anomaly for Mannheim. He was unable to provide even a vestigial argument linking Chiliasm either to the interests or the social position of those who held it. (6) If we read his account, however, another form of explanation does begin to suggest itself.

Chiliasm may be regarded as the product of ignorance and lack of organisation. If those who rebel against the impossible pressure of dominant institutions lack the models and competences required in social organisation, or perhaps even a conceptual scheme for explaining their predicament, Chiliastic responses are readily understood. Such groups can only look to their familiar personal relationships as models of social organisation, and lack the skills and resources which would be necessary actively to work for the downfall of their enemies and oppressors. Hence rebellious Russian peasantry seeking the 'Good Tsar', and the informal immediacy of the communities formed by the German Anabaptists whilst awaiting extermination.

The communities which sustained Calvinism were less lacking in cultural resources, and mobilised a greater range of competences in order to survive. They possessed what was required in the way of social organisation, and they knew how to sustain it. The Calvinists survived; the initially more numerous Anabaptists did not. Great numbers of the latter were to pour into cities of Calvinist or similar persuasion, there to be protected, organised, employed and converted. And great numbers were put to the sword. These different responses to external pressure, and their different fates, can only be properly understood in terms which involve consideration of the differential distribution of knowledge and institutional forms.

3 COMPETENCES AND RATIONALISATIONS

Although an adequate answer to the central problem of the chapter has yet to emerge, it is now clear that it is from Marx's broadly materialist perspective that we must proceed towards it. This perspective proved more satisfactory than Weber's, even when judged in the context of the latter's own empirical materials; its general social-psychological orientation proved the more apt. In Weber's idealist modes of analysis, men are held to act on the basis of general principles or values. Essentially, they are passive entities determined by the ideas they have absorbed; they are the instruments through which ideas bring about social change. In Marx, on the other hand, men generate ideas in response to practical exigiencies, and harness them to their service. If the ideas cease to serve men's interests they can be altered or cast aside; the active pursuit of interests brings about social change and determines the fate of ideas. All the evidence suggests that it is the latter view which provides the better schematic framework for the understanding of historical processes.

This is not to claim that Marx provides a comprehensive insight into individual psychology. Clearly he does not. Beliefs are not consciously appraised and related to interests in the course of every individual action; on the contrary, men tend to set beliefs and actions into routines, and operate with them unthinkingly most of the time. And it may well be that particular individuals sometimes give evidence of being incapable of deviating from and actively modifying the routinised courses of action upon which they rely. What Marx does is to identify the form of the relationship between men and their ideas and institutions which brings about social change as the cumulative consequence of its operation, and which accordingly has historical significance. It is often conveniently represented in an individualistic mode of speech by talking of the individual actor as someone who is a manipulator of his knowledge, and not the mere instrument of its application. But the use of this idiom of representation should not be taken to imply that detailed aspects of individual behaviour are being predicted. (7)

With this extremely important qualification, we can adopt what might be called the active model of man central to historical materialism, and explore what it implies about the potency of knowledge and ideas. We should assume then that men's actions are, in the long term, directed toward the fulfilment of needs and the furtherance of interests. It is this which gives action historical coherence, and not the determining power of knowledge and ideas. Knowledge, however, must still be treated as having potency and historical significance, since how activity can further an interest or fulfil a need is something which actors can only decide upon the basis of their knowledge, and what activities they are capable of performing is likewise a function of what they know. We must take our model as implying that action is decided upon by groups of actors *calculatively,* on the basis of what they know, to further their interests. This implies in turn that knowledge is a *resource,* and that its significance as an historical determinant stems precisely and only from its being a resource. (8)

The potential for successful action of any social group will
depend upon its skills and competences (its knowledge in the sense
of knowing how), and upon its knowledge of what appertains in its
social and physical setting (its knowledge in the sense of knowing
what). And it will depend too on the general distribution of
knowledge, in both these senses, in the group's entire society.
Actors themselves typically recognise this in their actions, and
operate with a mind to their skills and competences, and what might
be called their map of the social and physical landscape. Without in any way assuming that either kind of knowledge cannot be
modified, developed or improved, the existing immediate distribution of knowledge of both kinds must always be taken into account
in understanding social change in any particular context and period;
the state and distribution of knowledge is a necessary and
irreducible condition in the explanation of social change. (9)

It might be thought that there is an inconsistency here, that
one cannot argue both that men are restricted by the resources
of knowledge they possess, *and* that they are readily capable of
modifying and developing their knowledge at need. Unfortunately,
however, this awkward position is exactly what is empirically
indicated, and what we must be willing to accept. There are no
situations where existing instrumentally oriented knowledge could
not be developed and extended, and where the prompting of needs
and interests would not be capable of producing such changes. On
the other hand, it does not follow that men are capable of solving
all of the problems they set themselves simply by setting their
minds to it. (10) In historical studies of the natural sciences,
for example, it is clear that what scientists regard as satisfactory solutions to their problems frequently emerge, if they
emerge at all, at unpredictable intervals from the point when the
problems were first formulated and worked upon. Often such
solutions are the accidental by-products of work on another topic,
generated after direct attempts to find them have repeatedly become
deadlocked. If only because of this, because the problems men set
themselves may be intensely resistant to solution, the explanation of social change will never be able to by-pass consideration
of what is known by the actors bringing it about.

This stress on the essential historical significance of knowledge could be taken as contrary to the spirit of historical
materialism, the broad perspectives of which have, allegedly, been
guiding us. If this were so it would be of no importance, but I
do not think that, in fact, it is so. Although historical
materialism is frequently taken as claiming that knowledge is
derivative, epiphenomenal and superstructural, the high value which
Marx placed on technique, competence and what he regarded as
genuine knowledge surely suggests that this was not his position.
Avineri (1968) has produced convincing support for this suggestion
and indicated a more satisfactory interpretation of Marx's views
and terminology:

> according to Marx 'productive forces' are not objective facts
> external to human consciousness and human activity . . . the
> distinction between 'material base' and 'superstructure' is not
> a distinction between 'matter' and 'spirit' . . ., but between
> conscious human activity, aimed at the creation and preservation

of the conditions of human life, and human consciousness,
which furnishes reasons, rationalisations and modes of
legitimation and moral justification for the specific forms
that activity takes. (p. 76)

If we take it that knowledge which informs, or is realised in,
action is actually a constitutive part of what is referred to as
'conscious human activity', then Marx's position as interpreted
above becomes compatible with that being put forward here.   The
development, evaluation and utilisation of beliefs and representations as resources for the planning and execution of practical
activity has real historical significance from both perspectives.
And Marx's assertion that their development and utilisation as
legitimations has no such real independent significance is difficult
to oppose from the position taken here. Attempts to legitimate cannot stand as significant determinants of action: target audiences
cannot be expected passively to absorb them, accept them and
act upon the basis of them.   But neither do such attempts generate
representations of direct value as resources in activity.   Thus,
it is hard to discern how significant consequences can directly
derive from them. (11)

On this basis it is possible to make a partial and pragmatic
distinction between different kinds of knowledge.   Much knowledge
finds no application in the planning and execution of action, but
has been developed predominantly to provide legitimations,
justifications and 'ex post facto' rationalisations of activity.
In the academic context, it is found concentrated in such differentiated areas as philosophy, theology, political and ethical
theorising, and other fields notable for the propagation of
principles and maxims of conduct (which is not to say that everything in such fields is knowledge of this kind).   Such knowledge
can reasonably be referred to as a set of legitimations, and even
perhaps be usefully regarded as part of the 'superstructure' of
society.

But it must be emphasised that no fundamental distinctions can
be drawn between kinds of knowledge.   Beliefs and representations
are generated and given applications in an ongoing historical
process wherein, in different periods and contexts, they are
related to and modified by a whole range of diverse social and
instrumental interests.   They have no intrinsic properties, but
become labelled, say as legitimations or scientific statements,
according to how they are evaluated and used in particular situations.   And such labels cannot indicate with complete reliability
how, in the future, they will be employed as cultural resources.

It may be that we possess bodies of knowledge, systems of
beliefs and representations, which are no more than rationalising
structures, presently employed solely to furnish legitimations.
None the less, such structures are, as forms of culture or networks of concepts and relationships, entirely equivalent to other
such forms.   They are distinctive by virtue of the particular
social interests they are contingently related to, and the manner
in which they are actually deployed, but not by virtue of their
intrinsic character.   In themselves, they are typical organised
products of thought, and are thus available to actors as cultural
resources.   Hence, there is no 'a priori' reason why they should

not serve as models, or sources of organising principles, in the
speculative development of instrumentally significant knowledge.
There is indeed a considerable amount of evidence that some important innovations in the natural sciences have come about precisely
in this way, although what is less clear is how far such innovations would have been prevented or long-delayed if the particular
routes by which they were effected had not been available. (12)
Thus, we can assert with some confidence that rationalising
structures have been exploited as resources in the process of
scientific innovation, but we do not at present know how important
their influence has been upon the general trends of such innovation. (13)   Either way, however, rationalising structures must
be accepted as possible material causes of the growth of instrumental knowledge, even though their role in this respect is
necessarily unsystematic and unpredictable, and the extent of
their importance is unclear. (14)

Analogously, since legitimations and rationalisations are forms
of culture, they can be taken as *derivative* of other concurrently
existing social factors only in a restricted sense. The 'economic
foundation' of a society, or its 'conscious human activity', will
indeed shape its legitimations and rationalising structures, but it
cannot be taken as a sufficient cause of them; the character of
a society's rationalisations cannot be deduced from its structures
of activity. Rather, legitimations appropriate to given contexts
of activity will be constructed out of existing legitimations, and
existing cultural resources generally. A society's legitimations
must necessarily be understood by reference to its previously
given culture, and hence its *history*, as well as the immediate
context in which the legitimations are put forth. Indeed, quite
generally, a society at any point must be taken as a given whole,
fully intelligible only in terms of its history, and in which no
part is deducible from the other parts.

Thus, if one insists that a society be analysed into 'basic'
and 'derivative' elements, this should not be as a method of
explaining away some part of it; rather it should constitute an
attempt to locate the springs of change in the society, the areas
which generate precipitants of social change. (15) If society is
basically constituted of collectivities striving to sustain and
further their interests, then social change should be precipitated
by innovations which alter the resources, or the distribution of
the resources, available to the different collectivities for this
task. Precipitants of social change must be capable of being
used to further interests; they must make it possible for some
collectivity to *do* more, to achieve that which had been previously
impossible. Among such precipitants can be numbered newly dis-
covered or invented productive resources, new and improved skills
and techniques, changes in natural knowledge, newly evolved forms
of social organisation, and indeed practically any change in the
area of 'conscious human activity', wherein also instrumentally
applicable knowledge is included.

The changed possibilities for action which a particular innovation or transformation in this area generates frequently ensures
that it is institutionalised, and that it systematically engenders
further changes through the whole of the relevant society. The

innovation or transformation stands as a necessary cause of the
subsequent more general social changes, although the detailed
character of these subsequent changes is only fully intelligible
in terms of the initial state of the 'conscious human activity'
in the society: this initial state is a necessary condition of
the subsequent changes.

In contrast, changes in the derivative, superstructural features
of a society, in forms of legitimation and rationalisation, expressive symbols and the like, cannot be expected to result in more
general social change. Such features are not sources of competence;
nor (except in the very indirect and unpredictable way mentioned
above) do they assist or facilitate interest furthering activity.
Thus, the superstructure of a society with its rationalisations
and legitimations will systematically respond and adjust to changes
in the base, in 'conscious human activity'; but the converse
will not be true.

4 GENERAL CONCLUSIONS

Our examination of the traditional problems of the sociology of
knowledge from the general standpoint outlined in the opening
chapter is now at an end. Hopefully, a reasonably coherent picture
of the implications of that standpoint will have emerged, and an
adequate indication of how the sociology of knowledge should
proceed. It is true that no laws or necessary connections are
proposed to link knowledge and the social order, and that no abstract
instructions are set out for the investigation and explanation of
bodies of knowledge. But the basic claim that knowledge is a
resource in activity and not a direct determinant of it makes such
an approach inappropriate. And in any case recommended investi-
gatory procedures and forms of explanation can be at least as
successfully communicated by direct reference to concrete examples,
serving as direct models of procedure, as by the production of
abstract accounts. The great merit of the best achievements in
the sociology of knowledge, of much of Marx's work and Goldmann's
analysis of literature and philosophy, is precisely that they can
be taken up directly, and used as models in further investigations
which can in turn add to our understanding. Knowledge can develop
in immediate moves from concrete instance to concrete instance as
well as by the extension of abstract theoretical structures. (16)

At the same time, there is probably much to be gained by examining the formal difficulties which doubtless exist in the theoretical
position taken here, and by continuing to extend it in so far as
that is possible. One of my main concerns has been to show how
the possibilities of the sociology of knowledge will increase as
does our understanding of the nature of human interests and of
social structure. Investigation and controversy centred upon
these concepts has always lain at the heart of sociology and
doubtless will continue to do so. The significance and relationship of 'objective' and 'subjective' conceptions of social structure,
and of 'real', 'perceived' and 'misperceived' interests, are matters
of great sociological importance concerning which any kind of consensus is likely to emerge, if at all, only after many more years

of unsettled and wide-ranging argument. For this reason, I have deliberately refrained from advancing any precise definitions of 'interest' and 'social structure'; this would have had the effect of linking the claims being advanced to particular schools of thought within sociological theory. Instead, I have been content, as it were, to latch the sociology of knowledge into the ongoing general trends of sociological thought.

Simply to acknowledge the central importance of the concepts of interest and social structure is, however, to indicate a leaning to the standpoint of historical materialism. And I do indeed regard the broad features of that standpoint as among the best possible starting points for the development of the sociology of knowledge and sociological theory generally. But it would be wrong for me to attempt to situate this work within the general tradition of historical materialism. However much it agrees formally with the assumptions of materialism, and however much it deviates from the empiricist presuppositions typical of the Anglo-Saxon orientation to the social sciences, it is in the latter context that fundamentally it belongs. Historical materialism has been accepted here only in so far as it has merits as an entirely naturalistic account of man's activity and its historical development; whereas the development of historical materialism itself has proceeded mainly on the basis of teleological, or other avowedly evaluative or non-naturalistic presuppositions. (17)

Writing from a firmly naturalistic perspective, I have found myself opposed to many empiricist accounts of how knowledge is actually created and sustained; to this extent I have found empiricism naturalistically inadequate. But as a tradition it seems to me to express some well-conceived ideals and aspirations. It is fashionable today to dismiss these ideals, as expressed in such notions as the value-neutrality of knowledge, and to hold instead that knowledge should be developed and constructed so that it explicitly sustains and reinforces the evaluations and aspirations of particular social groupings. Evidently the advocates of such positions find it desirable that future learning should be so heavily dependent on current, fallible assessments of value, of interest, and of the means of furthering interest. Surely it is a preferable, if less realistic, ideal to seek to know before one judges, to seek to minimise the need for rationalisations of particular interests as a component in the construction of knowledge, and to seek to express 'the intention of a good life' in well-informed and well-constructed activity.

NOTES

CHAPTER 1 THE PROBLEM OF KNOWLEDGE

1 It is these metaphors which Mannheim uses to make some of his
most radical criticisms of existing conceptions of knowledge.
Rather than attacking the predominantly individualistic and contemplative epistemologies of his time in terms of his explicit
alternative conception, we find him instead resorting to a more
sophisticated usage of the same contemplative standpoint. Take,
for example, his treatment of the diverse, apparently mutually
incompatible, views of a society, characteristically associated with
its different social classes or sub-cultures. The usual way of
accounting for these in contemplative terms was to hold that since
there was only one reality with which verbal accounts could correspond, only one such account, at most, could be correct. The other,
incorrect, accounts would probably be ideologies generated in
response to social interests. Mannheim applies contemplative conceptions in a more sophisticated way, employing a pictorial metaphor
to advantage. We are told to look at a physical object and consider
what we see. It will be a partial view of the object, a particular
perspective depending upon our particular position with respect to
the object. If we found other observers, working from different
standpoints, in possession of completely different conceptions or
perspectives, we should not assume that those perspectives were
erroneous simply because they differed from our own. Why then
should we not treat different conceptions of society as the products
of different standpoints and acknowledge that all of them may have
value, or as Mannheim would say, limited validity? And why should
we not recognise that we can learn from all the different perspectives, just as we can learn more and more about a physical object
by observing it from different standpoints (cf. Mannheim (1936),
ch. 5, pt 4)?
2 A parallel discussion of perception should, ideally, accompany
this discussion of representation. We do indeed learn to see
the world in terms of meaningful symbols - as assemblages of culturally meaningful components. The raw material gathered by our
senses is actively processed and schematised before it becomes
perceived sensation. Perception is selective: we see in terms of

the interests which affect us directly, or indirectly through their
effect on our socialisation.

3 Every representation can be put to two kinds of use. It can be
routinely applied, in conjunction with the procedures into which
it fits, to any of the ends for which the procedure is routinely
appropriate. And it can be taken itself as a cultural resource
in the generation of new knowledge, just as it was made from
previous cultural resources (cf. Kuhn, Postscript, 1970, for a
discussion). Normally, the former is the institutionalised usage
and the latter an occasional variant. But in science the reverse
can sometimes be the case, and this is what accounts for the
particular problems alluded to here.

4 Ivins (1953) notes that when the camera first came into use
there was much interest in 'photographic distortion'. This interest
only declined as we allowed the camera to define our idea of
accurate representation.

Photographs appear infrequently in scientific textbooks. They
play a significant role in some astronomical and geological works
and occasionally in biology. But, given their cheapness in
production, what Ivins calls their 'exact repeatability', and
their elimination of much personal idiosyncracy from the illustra-
tive process, it is perhaps initially surprising that they are
not used more. The probable reason for this is that other illus-
trative techniques offer much greater possibilities for intervention
in the process of manufacture. The esoteric theories and abstractions of science necessitate esoteric ways of seeing and highly
schematic illustration. It is the diagram which reigns supreme
in physics and chemistry texts, and plays a major role elsewhere.

5 It is interesting to note how people intuitively translate their
awareness of the *conventions* of a pictorial representation into
a statement of how *realistic* it is. Thus, Daniel Gasman (1971)
reproduces some drawings of marine organisms by the German
scientist-philosopher Ernst Haeckel and comments:

> they are not quite objectively rendered and the information
> they are supposed to convey is hardly neutral. Their orna-
> mental lay-out and hypertrophied patterning, and the fantastic
> and bizarre look of the unfamiliar flora and fauna, transform
> them in the direction of disquieting, even nightmarish repre-
> sentations that seem to be related to the type of naturalistic
> mysticism which can be observed in late nineteenth-century Art
> Nouveau and symbolist artists like Obvist and Redon. (pp. 73-4)

It is clear that Gasman could not have checked with the organisms
themselves - the 'reality' in question. His opinion derives from
the conventions of the drawings he reproduces in his book. Their
sinuous lines, heavy contrast, directional lighting, stressed
planes of symmetry and implied upward motion are far from our
presently accepted conventions of scientific representation, and
have typically been used to convey, in the art of Western cultures,
profundity and emotional intensity. It remains, none the less, an
intriguing question as to why Haeckel chose to employ these conventions in a 'scientific' work; Gasman was right to find the
drawings interesting.

6 For science as a craft skill cf. Polanyi (1958), Ravetz (1971),
For a discussion of the detailed relationship of diagrams, and

competences or 'techniques of inference', in science cf. Toulmin
(1953).

7   Cf. Bloor (1973, 1976). It is interesting that some people,
impressed with the power of mathematical knowledge and puzzled as
to its origin, have claimed that there exists a world of mathematical objects, accessible to thought. The knowledge is thus
provided with a reality to which it can correspond.

8   This very important point is either explicitly accepted by the
writers discussed in the next section, or is compatible with their
work. Habermas has perspicaciously discussed Marx's position on
this matter, showing how he retained a belief in the primacy of
'external nature' even as he held that man made his world in the
process of work (1972, pt 1.2).

9   Two general points are worth bearing in mind about Lukács's
account. First, wherever possible, Lukács talks of consciousness
and its determinants rather than of knowledge. He prefers to
think in terms of active mental processes rather than in terms of
the nature of knowledge; in this he is at the opposite extreme
to Habermas. And indeed the question of the relationship of
mental processes and the hypothesised knowledge on the basis of
which they proceed is a topic of great complexity and fascination.
But it would not be correct to imagine that Lukács, like some
modern ethnomethodologists, considered knowledge as a term which
merely reifies consciousness, and misleads however it is used. It
is perfectly in order to talk of Lukács's account of the character
of knowledge.

   Second, Lukács was primarily concerned with men's understanding
of social reality, and rarely considered natural knowledge. He
did, none the less, include natural science within the ambit of
his views, and purported to have exposed the inadequacies of its
method. Lukács was, however, monumentally ignorant of scientific
practice and, against his own precepts, equated natural science
with the abstractions of positivist philosophy; hence we have the
absurdities of his vituperations against science.

10 Lukács's account was eschatological in character. A total
understanding of reality would eventually be achieved by the
proletariat. This element of Lukács's thought, with its obvious
and well-documented inadequacies, will not be discussed here,
although doubtless his desire to demonstrate and justify the
historical role of the proletariat influenced his work at many
levels.

11 Consider, for example, another important theme in Lukács's
'History and Class-Consciousness' (1923) - that, since our knowledge is of a changing, man-influenced reality, it must itself
perpetually change. Clearly there is some point to this claim:
if we were to change the rules of chess, our knowledge of how to
play the game well would change: if a laissez-faire economy were
slowly to metamorphose into monopoly capitalism, many associated
economic rules and theories would doubtless be modified: if the
last remaining giant pandas were to be exterminated, doubtless
our catalogues of existing fauna would be adjusted accordingly.
But what justifies giving this relationship general significance?
After all, for over two millennia the central techniques and
descriptive categories of Euclidean geometry and Archimedean

mechanics have been found applicable and acceptable in diverse societies.   Do not people seek to embody in their knowledge principles which they find in a sense invariant over a wide range of contexts, applicable to systems even during change?   Is not much knowledge precisely knowledge of what is involved in change? A changing reality only *implies* the transient character of knowledge generally on the assumption that knowledge copies or reflects reality at a superficial level.   Yet Lukács made the implication and made much of it.   Ironically, it was one of the components in Lukács's attack upon science which he conceived of as a reified body of knowledge seeking to pass off contingent facts of present reality as manifestations of eternal laws.   The practice of natural science is in fact thoroughly dialectical.

12   Habermas's discussions of Marx's and Pierce's epistemologies are especially rewarding.

13   Habermas does not interrupt the flow of his text with examples. And, indeed, to illustrate his case convincingly, as it can be, would be a lengthy task in the context of most scientific fields. There are, however, some fields, like cartography, which are sufficiently accessible to 'outsiders' and provide immediate and intuitively satisfying support for Habermas's account.   If one can see how an atlas is the product of various instrumental interests, rather than of undirected contemplation, and how it is communally sustained as a repository of knowledge, one has an excellent concrete model of how Habermas's account can treat of knowledge generally.

14   Had the interest of this book been primarily epistemological, it would have been necessary to emphasise the differences between Habermas's and traditional instrumentalist epistemologies (cf. Habermas. 1973).   Habermas's own interest is itself primarily epistemological;   like Lukács his primary goal is the refutation of 'positivism' and the construction of an alternative form of 'self-understanding' for the sciences.   Unfortunately, in doing so, he retains far too much of the 'positivism' he criticises.

15   Habermas is clear that KCIs emerged in the course of man's natural history, during the self-constituting evolutionary process which is both our past, and our present condition.   But he makes little further progress in characterising this emergence. KCIs cannot be considered entirely as the products of cultural evolution;   for culturally defined rules, problems and standards appear as such only within frames of reference defined by KCIs themselves.   On the other hand, Habermas is most anxious that KCIs should not be considered entirely by thinking of 'reason as an organ of adaptation' or knowledge as an instrument of adaptation to a changing environment.   He ends by asserting that KCIs derive both from nature (biologically evolved cognitive capacities?) and from the cultural break with nature (cf. Habermas, (1972), pp. 312, 196-7).

16   For Habermas 'practical' implies a contrast with 'technical': it is taken in its Germanic sense to imply 'moral' or 'ethical', usually with reference to the political context.

17   Habermas's ideal of self-reflective knowledge will not be considered further here.   A detailed critique would follow the same lines as, and emerge as isomorphous with, the discussion of

the hermeneutic ideal which follows in the main text.

18 A formulation, or reformulation, of this kind seems to be implied in Habermas (1973).

19 Among the work illustrating the consensual character of science, that of T. S. Kuhn (1970) is most noteworthy. For the indexical character of scientific knowledge and its context-dependence cf. Barnes and Law (1976). A general discussion of the social character of natural scientific knowledge with further references to concrete studies is Barnes (1974).

20 To say this is not to propose an alternative explanation to that which relates Habermas's views to expedient social interests. It is frequently and plausibly suggested that Habermas is a humanist intellectual, responding to the threat of redundancy as the scope of the technique of natural science is extended. Realising that to attack the validity of natural science itself is an unrealistic strategy in the modern world, he seeks to limit its scope and assert its subservience, in the last analysis, to the field of learning he himself represents. Hence he attacks scientistic philosophy and what he considers to be the extension of science into the realm of human affairs. Since Habermas's views are strongly criticised here, it is perhaps worth noting that I share his suspicion of the growth of certain quantitative methods in the social sciences: systems analysis, econometrics, cybernetics and the rest. Much of this material (although certainly not all) is worse than useless. But it does not represent the extension of natural scientific techniques. Its techniques, like its interests, spring from a different source. They are, however, usually legitimated by reference to some extreme form of positivist philosophy of science, and, as elsewhere, Habermas fails to make the essential distinction between philosophy of science and natural science itself.

21 It follows from this view that reference to the 'disinterested evaluation' of knowledge is in most contexts a harmless enough formulation, which can be taken as practically equivalent to 'evaluation in terms of an authentic interest in prediction and control'.

22 In some spheres, notably natural science, an attempt is made to enforce the transmission of one message only, presumably to minimise the effects of crossover distortion. There is no 'a priori' reason why such an attempt should not succeed and produce an entirely non-evaluative information flow. If this occurred in a natural science it could be legitimately said to be non-evaluative in a certain restricted sense. Its discourse and knowledge would, of course, still be sustained socially and would remain normative in that sense. The electrical metaphor is useful again, in distinguishing these two senses in which science can be said to be normative. To talk of the normative component, in one sense, is like talking of the visual information in a TV signal - information which could be entirely eliminated to leave the sound only. To talk of the normative component in the second sense is to talk of the conventions in the code which is used to convey *any* information by the TV signal: there must always be such conventions, but to an extent they are a matter of choice and agreement.

23   Much the same view of knowledge generation is found in Bhaskar (1975). Where I emphasise the instrumental features of the account by talking of cultural resources, Bhaskar, who is a realist, uses Aristotelean terminology and talks of material causes or transitive objects of knowledge. But the terms are substantially equivalent.

24   For a discussion of pictorial representation in science which deals with both cultural resources and instrumental interests cf. Rudwick (1976).

25   Thus, Habermas, whose perception is dependent upon the tradition of epistemological writing, argues that there is only one possible natural science; it is not, as Marcuse would have it, a historical project which could be different. In doing so he remains unaware of the material causes of scientific knowledge, and talks vaguely of science as 'pure instrumentality'.

Popper's early epistemology (1934) is, in contrast, engagingly direct upon these matters. In the terms it specifies, rational men can indeed hold to diverse bodies of knowledge; there is little restriction on the nature of what can be rationally believed. Popper's epistemology does not identify the best knowledge but the most rational men. Moreover, it identifies the most rational men in *conventional* terms, not in absolute ones; Popper is clear that his epistemological standards have only the standing of conventions. Hence, Popper provides us with no naturalistic basis upon which to differentiate and evaluate knowledge claims. His position is just as relativistic in its implications as that which follows here. The truly remarkable thing is how rarely this is noted (cf. Barnes, 1976).

26   Another possibility, not discussed here, is to assert the progressive nature of knowledge, and the possibility of differentially evaluating different knowledge claims, on purely instrumental grounds. The best knowledge is that which enables its possessors to *do* the most, to achieve their ends the most successfully. Unfortunately, there seems no easy way of applying this criterion, since different cultures possess different competences and seek different ends. It would appear necessary to set prior evaluations upon different aims and activities before an instrumental assessment of knowledge claims could be carried out (just as later in the text we find that prior evaluations of real universals are essential before a realist assessment of knowledge claims can be carried out). It remains an empirical possibility that men in all cultures would, on acquaintance, admit the superior instrumental efficacy of western science. But this does not effect the thesis that different knowledge claims should stand symmetrically for sociological purposes.

27   Bhaskar, whose (1975) was the model for the foregoing argument, recognises this conclusion by acknowledging that there is no way of avoiding epistemological relativism.

28   Cf. Polanyi (1958), Wilson (1971), Horton and Finnegan (1973), Barnes (1974).

29   The relevant ethnomethodological literature is too well known to need citing here, but references to the interaction view, which is less familiar to sociologists, can be found in Barnes (1974). The interaction view is applied to science in Hesse (1974), and

an indication of the applicability of the notion of indexicality
to scientific expressions is given in Barnes and Law (1976).
30   I believe it also to be the case that knowledge everywhere is
based upon the same range of shared cognitive propensities. If
there is indeed such a psychic unity among men, it reinforces the
case for treating all institutionalised beliefs symmetrically
as knowledge.
31   The general cognitive processes involved in knowledge generation cannot be considered here. A stimulating attempt to formulate
them and exemplify their operation is Hesse (1974).
32   Analogously, moral and evaluative beliefs are doubtless modifi-
able by primitive causal inputs with a real basis. Evaluations and
ethical views are no more immune to change with changing experience
than are descriptive views. Nor are they any more varied and
diverse. Curiously, moral relativism is much easier to accept today
than descriptive relativism (Lukes, 1974). But the arguments for
and against are identical in both cases. On the one hand, alternative beliefs are rationally possible, and actually found, in both
cases. On the other hand, in neither case is belief so arbitrary
and uninfluenced by real primitive causes that we can choose to
believe whatever we like. Actions we can choose; beliefs,
strangely, we cannot. We cannot simply decide to believe that
bullets are harmless, nor that child killing is every man's duty.
We could say as much, but our actions would betray us in both cases.
(Needless to say, both the above are believable, and have been
believed, in other contexts, but however one develops the argument
the essential symmetry between the two cases remains.)

CHAPTER 2 THE PROBLEM OF IDEOLOGY

1   The enduring value of these is apparent in the extent to which
they have been taken up even by liberal academics; cf. Halévy
(1928), whose penetrating analysis of the development of philosophical radicalism expands across its five hundred pages without
once citing Marx.
2   Cf. the way Marx (1969) contrasts the rationalisations of
Malthus with the 'scientific honesty' of Ricardo.
3   'The market', and 'the arm' with which it will shortly be compared, and, indeed, most of the representations of the natural
sciences can all confidently be labelled 'ideal-types' without fear
of contradicting Weber's formal definition.
4   If we give it this sense, then we can accept Mannheim's insight
that the genesis of beliefs has much to tell us about the extent of
their validity.
5   The relationship of knowledge and social structure is, needless
to say, a most important topic and will be discussed at length in
Chapter 3. The terminological decision taken here will in no way
handicap the later discussion.
6   Contradiction can persist in any mode of thought; arguably it
does persist in all systems of knowledge. Conversely, any number
of particular beliefs or knowledge-claims can always be arranged
coherently together so that, formally, they are logically compatible.
Hence, the consistency of an existing set of beliefs is, in the last

analysis, no more than a matter of style. Beliefs can appear
perfectly consistent and still be held to be ideologically determined, and vice versa. It remains the case that perceived inconsistency in texts, where formal consistency is often sought for,
offers a clue to or indication of the possible existence of
ideological determination.

7 Even beliefs which develop entirely as rationalisations, or as
indicators of conformity and social affiliation, constitute no
exception to the above remarks. Typically, they are represented
in ways which deny their true provenance; major rationalisations
may, for example, be held to derive entirely from religious
revelation, or from logic alone.

  Professions of belief which do no more than express conformity
are scarcely touched upon in this book despite their wide occur-
rences and the many intriguing features they display. They are
probably best discussed in conjunction with styles of dress and
coiffure and other forms of expressive symbolism, as in Douglas
(1970).

8 For a discussion of these points cf. Barnes (1974), pp. 128 ff.

9 It remains perfectly feasible none the less to regard a particular knowledge claim as valid, yet as ideologically determined
in most contexts. And as a matter of everyday practice it would
seem wise to keep matters of validity and matters of naturalistic
explanation separate. One might, for example, regard a new
argument against hereditarian accounts of racial differences in
intelligence as powerful and justified, yet, at the same time,
relate its rapid acceptance to concealed social interests.

10 Indeed, the essential difference between this kind of check
and the check we would make before, say, accepting a mathematical
proof is a remarkably minor one. In the former case we explore
whether another actor, programmed in a certain way, would come to
a certain belief or not, in the latter we explore whether we
ourselves would do so!

11 Mathematics is here being treated as a set of conventions just
like any other knowledge. This is necessary if the symmetrical
sociological approach to knowledge advocated earlier is to be sustained. But it does not, as some might think, put that approach
under any strain. Routine mathematical procedure or inference is
not a matter of following logical rules, or of being constrained
by necessary truths. It is the product of the open-ended following of conventions, cf. Bloor (1973, 1976).

12 For examples, including the debates over water-fluoridation,
tobacco and lung cancer, and the alleged harmful effects of
cannabis, cf. Barnes (1974), ch. 6.

13 The requirements of concealed interests may of course be met
by the indications of accepted knowledge, including science. One
would then expect the fortunate beneficiaries to transmit and
disseminate the knowledge as much as possible. The question of
'why' a particular individual believes that which he wants to
believe, when he hears it from a source he genuinely trusts, or
substantiated by evidence he genuinely finds compelling, is,
however, a psychological question we shall not attempt to answer
here.

14 This is the reason why so much weight was given to departures

from 'normal practice' and naturally reasonable procedure in the preceding section of this chapter.

15   The reader can probably think of many similar examples in sociology and economics. In the natural sciences cf. Rudwick (1972), Coleman (1970), MacKenzie and Barnes (1975), and more speculatively, Forman (1971). The general argument here may usefully be compared with that of Elias (1971).

16   For some account of the history of Euclidean geometry and its treatment in different cultures cf. Heath (1925).

17   There are a number of absurdities which can be 'proved' in fine Euclidean style by starting with slightly inaccurately drawn diagrams. But the standard presentation of Euclid does not seek to establish the credentials of any of the drawings actually used in proofs.

18   Professional mathematicians would indeed probably want to reject as unsound the entire body of mathematical lore routinely transmitted in educational systems. Yet this is the predominant institutional form of mathematical knowledge. Nor are mathematicians necessarily any more content with their own sophisticated demonstrations. Often they appear to simultaneously believe in the rigour of their knowledge and in its inadequacy. Thus, Forder (1927) in his axiomatisation: 'the virtue of a logical proof is not that it compels belief, but that it suggests doubts' (viii). Many mathematicians evidently grasp in their own way, in the idiom of their own thought, what is referred to here, in the present idiom, as the conventional character of mathematical knowledge.

19   Forder (1927, viii) hints at a clash of scholarly and pedagogical interests when he writes:

> teachers of elementary Geometry and writers of elementary
> text-books can learn from [my book] how far short of logical
> perfection are the proofs usually received; and this should
> result in an improvement of Geometrical teaching, unless indeed
> it be contended that an unsound proof has an educational value
> not possessed by a sound one.

It would seem that this contention did have something in it.

20   For a discussion of why certain forms of mathematical demonstration might be sustained by more general interest in social control cf. Shapin and Barnes (1977).

21   None of the above should be taken as criticism of the Euclidean tradition. To emphasise how its knowledge has varied over time is merely to note something which appertains to any knowledge-bearing tradition, although admittedly it does have the accidental effect of making justification of the knowledge that much more difficult. It might be thought that too much stress has been put on this variation, and that in Euclidean geometry there are captured certain enduring, timelessly valuable, relationships. There is however a problem in deciding what might sensibly be treated as stable in the development of Euclidean geometry, and in what way it should be valued. In what respects is original Euclid the same as axiomatised Euclid? And wherein resides the value of what they have in common? These are fascinating and important problems well worth pursuing; but it is worth noting how numerous and intractable have been the disagreements of those who have addressed them.

CHAPTER 3 THE PROBLEM OF IMPUTATION

1   The sociology of knowledge as practiced in the USA has been notably empiricist and individualistic in character, in comparison with the European work which initially inspired it, cf. Curtis and Petras (1970). It is sometimes said that this reflects the removal of the field of study from its initial involvement with political issues and the explicitly polemical literature of Marxism. Needless to say, however, the US literature in the sociology of knowledge is not noticeably less political in its orientation than its European counterpart. Feuer is no more a disinterested scholar than was Lukács. He expresses his political convictions with an extraordinary nineteenth century self-confidence, contrasting the 'empirical' work of those he approves with the 'ideological' outpourings of others. Thus, his work possesses an antique charm which quite disarms serious criticism. Cf, the following on Adam Smith:

> [Smith and Ricardo] wrote books of clearly stated propositions which could be verified or falsified by empirical facts; . . . Smith did once speak of the 'invisible hand' as guiding the interaction of individual economic decisions to promote the general welfare. . . . But there was no mythological element in Smith's analysis. He traced the verifiable, observable components in the causal chains of economic decisions and their consequences, and in his pleasure that the process culminated in a higher well-being, he used the metaphor of an eighteenth century optimist, the 'invisible hand'. (1975, pp. 166-7)

2 Feuer is not well disposed toward these groups of intellectuals; among their typical shortcomings, we are told, are sexual sadism, anti-feminism, authoritarianism and masochism.

3   Such problems have been made the basis for a radical critique of the view that knowledge has a continuing existence in a society as an entity in its own right. This critique, developed by ethno-methodologists such as Pollner and Zimmermann cannot be discussed here. If it were accepted, a total fragmentation of what we regard as culture would be implied, with the consequence that imputation problems would cease to exist altogether. Beliefs and ideas would become 'occasioned products' lacking duration in time and connected solely (and mysteriously) with the immediate context in which they arose, cf. J. Douglas (1970).

4   The only such accounts with which I am familiar both derive from Wittgenstein's work. The ethnomethodologists have approached the problem via his treatment of following a rule. Mary Hesse (1974) has incorporated his resemblance theory of universals into traditional empiricist treatments of inductive inference, with what to some philosophers are radical consequences.

5   The term 'interest' has no particular theoretical value for Feuer and he avoids using it, presumably because of its socio-logical significance. There seems to be nothing in Feuer's account, however, which would debar the use of the term.

6   The 'situated' character of such an imputation must be stressed as strongly as possible. As was pointed out earlier Feuer rightly rejects the view that ideas or beliefs can be inherently those of a class, or even a group of intellectuals.

7 As in any other area of modern culture, there is, in natural science, a strand of individualistic, atomistic, reductionist thinking. It is indeed an important and productive strand. Many working molecular biologists, for example, tend to be extraordinarily atomistic and reductionist in their cognitive style, and in the way they evaluate the work of others.

8 I have stressed this point at some length since so many sociologists, on both sides of methodological controversies about individualism, seem to accept, wrongly, that a choice has to be made between individualistic empiricism, and metaphysics or holistic speculation.

9 Given that structural hypotheses often present daunting technical difficulties when they come to be empirically tested it is worth noting that individualistic hypotheses also present their problems. Certainly, in the matter of testing some of his own hypotheses, Feuer makes an interesting contrast with his own rhetoric upon the virtues of empiricism.

10 At this point, the possibilities of the sociology of knowledge are bound up with our developing understanding of social structure, and can only be expounded further if a stand is taken upon some particular theory of social structure. My own convictions in this area go no further than the view that structural theories of society are justified.

11 A further contrast relevant to the following discussion is that between Pearson's idiosyncratic but none the less demanding positivism, which judged Mendelism for the most part as unscientific speculative theorising, and Bateson's less systematic holistic-idealist view of science. Their respective positions evoke Mannheim's contrast of 'natural law' and 'conservative' thought (1953).

12 Where, during an extended training, scientists have laboriously acquired particular skills and techniques, there is a tendency for them to advocate theories which imply an important role for those techniques. In the present dispute biologists trained in experimental techniques tended to the Mendelian view, which indicated an important role for breeding experiments in scientific research. But despite this, and some other relationships between competence and theoretical preference, the evidence suggests that this kind of effect was not the major factor in sustaining the controversy (cf. MacKenzie and Barnes, 1975).

13 As in many cases such as this, there was also an intimate cultural connection between the esoteric scientific context and the general social context. Thus, for Karl Pearson gradualism was more or less a cosmological principle, and his deployment of gradualist explanation in both the esoteric technical spheres of his work and as an account of social change in his political polemics, created a situation where his 'findings' in the two areas were mutually reinforcing, and each could be treated as evidence of the soundness of the other.

14 Cf. Coleman (1970, p. 295). Coleman establishes the connection between William Bateson's scientific theories and his political views, which are shown to be 'conservative' in the sense defined by Mannheim (1953). The discussion here, and in MacKenzie and Barnes (1975), also assumes this denotation of the term

'conservative' and implies nothing, for example, about formal political doctrines or affiliations.

15   The controversy should not be regarded as an isolated and esoteric case, nor the interests invoked to make it intelligible as rare sources of disturbance of scientific thought.   From before Napoleonic wars until 1914 such interests frequently modulated scientific debate, in the geological and palaeontological controversies of the early century and later the controversy over evolution, in physiology and medicine, and in physics and chemistry too.   Although the particular example was selected partly because of my own familiarity with the concrete materials concerning it, it also typifies an important set of instances where instrumentally oriented thought is heavily modulated by major socially structured patterns of interest.

16   It is worth noting how some years later Mendelism became characterised as a typical manifestation of bourgeois thought, particularly in the struggle between Soviet geneticists and supporters of Lysenko.

17   Strictly speaking one needs to add a 'ceteris paribus' clause here and at some further points, since it is conceivable, even if highly unlikely, that other constellations of particular interests could have sustained an identical set of controversial issues.

18   This is not to say that the two movements themselves would have disappeared.   Unlike ethical codes, such as the mediaeval rules of chivalry, knowledge, with its directly instrumental dimension, does not necessarily decline when the particular interests bearing upon it are eliminated;   instead it is generally modified into a more straightforwardly instrumental form.   Biometry and Mendelism could continue (and did continue) as intellectual traditions, in the absence of the particular interests which sustained the controversy between them.

19   Modern hereditarian thought in the social sciences and psychology, although often loosely associated with political conservatism, is very much the intellectual progeny of the positivism of the biometricians, and does not stand in any close relationship with the tenets of Mendelism as it first existed in Britain.

20   One of the most interesting and detailed studies of the individual situations and beliefs of people involved in putatively ideologically determined debate is Harwood's recent work on the Jensen controversy (1976-7).   This material illustrates the value of the study of individual beliefs and characteristics.   And the author's admirably disinterested treatment of his material permits an assessment of the utility of constructing profiles of the types of individual most likely to be on one or other side of the race/IQ debate.   My own assessment is that such profiles should be taken mainly as circumstantial evidence for general structurally based hypotheses concerning the causes of the debate.

21   An alternative way of putting this, which some people will prefer, is to say that we achieve accounts of the existence and operation of social structures by making references to particular actions and utterances.

22   This statement holds in two ways.   It is true of the methodology of MacKenzie and Barnes (1975) and MacKenzie (1976);

much of the material in these papers was made available by Mac-
Kenzie's detailed study of Karl Pearson's work and career.   And
it is true of the body of excellent historical work which exists
in this area, and which is referenced in detail in the above
papers.
23   For more extensive biographical material cf. Coleman (1970)
and MacKenzie and Barnes (1975).
24   Unusual combinations of beliefs and activities in particular
individuals do frequently occasion surprise in the social sciences,
and sometimes evoke 'explanations' of individual 'irrationality'.
But such instances are generally nothing more than evidence of
parochialism and lack of insight on the part of investigators.
Thus, although his thought is often a cause for puzzlement, there
was nothing particularly inconsistent or otherwise peculiar in
the beliefs of the hereditarian communist J. B. S. Haldane.
25   The mechanism whereby initial institutional affiliations can
influence further ones is plausibly delineated in Becker (1960,
1964).
26   There is a formal problem of deciding how far the materials
examined by Goldmann can be called knowledge.   Racine's plays
clearly cannot, but I have restricted discussion here to Goldmann's
treatment of Pascal and Jansenist doctrine, and simply made the
provisional decision to treat them as a body of publicly sustained
beliefs.
27   According to Goldmann's criteria, the 'officiers' almost, but
not quite, constituted a genuine social class (cf. Goldmann (1964),
pp. 119-20).
28   Many points of this analysis are disputed, and the relevant
empirical evidence is admittedly inconclusive.   For the terminology
used cf. p. 419.
29   How precisely the ideology served the interests is not made
entirely clear in 'The Hidden God'.   It is emphasised however that
Jansenism and the practice of withdrawal *were* regarded as a major
political threat to the monarchy despite the apparently quiescent
form of opposition they encouraged, and that they attracted retri-
bution more severe in many instances than that meted out to active
opposition groups.
30   Indeed, Goldmann's clear awareness of the way that the Jansenist
doctrine was built from existing cultural material makes his discussion relevant to some of the earlier themes of this book.   He
notes how the physical cosmology of Jansenism was taken from
Descartes, and how its 'Augustinian' doctrine was not so much
provided by Jansen for the movement as taken and adapted to serve
interests quite different from those which can be attributed to its
originator.
31   For example, having located support for Jansenism among
'officiers' and a discontented minority of the upper aristocracy,
Goldmann goes on to associate the ideology entirely with the
interests of the former group.   The latter he treats as a dis-
affected minority, without the power to act autonomously and hence
reduced to an expedient alliance which involved a sympathetic
response to the ideas of the ally (cf. Goldmann (1964), pp. 115-17).
32   Goldmann ranges even wider in his discussion of the social
incidence of 'tragedies of refusal', the aesthetic analogues of
ideologies of withdrawal.

33 Goldmann's own general views on imputation problems are set out in Chapter 1, and are reasserted throughout the text. His specific treatment of historical materials is exemplified in Chapter VI, and of biographical material in Chapter VIII and Appendix A. His evaluation of individualistic criticism is well illustrated by the extended footnote on pp. 103-5. All this material is worth serious study in so far as it bears upon problems of imputation.

34 Rightly, Goldmann distinguishes the real logical coherence of material from its merely formal properties and presentation:

> Too much clarity darkens, wrote Pascal, and I have preferred genuine clarity to any purely formal and apparent clarity. (1964, x)

35 Goldmann does indeed present a compelling vision of continuous cultural development from Cartesian rationalism through Pascal's tragic vision to dialectical materialism. But from the perspective of the present volume this is possible because of the use made of earlier culture in the development of new, and not because the earlier form was set on a path of progress toward the new.

36 Thus, for example, those who explain science as a progressive movement of belief into closer and closer correspondence with objective reality scarcely ever expose the teleological character of their thought.

37 Several of the generalisations which follow are not explicitly set out by Goldmann, but they are of assistance in conveying a condensed account of his argument and might reasonably be thought to be implicit in his position.

38 Goldmann sees this concept as the logical endpoint of Jansenist doctrine (cf. Goldmann (1964), Chapter VII).

39 It may well be that the peculiarly perfect isomorphism between social structure and ideological structure which Goldmann makes apparent has, as he suggests, a particular aesthetic importance, and can be taken as part of the explanation of the enduring aesthetic and literary value of Pascal's and Racine's works. But this important point need not be made in a teleological, evaluative idiom.

40 Among the Zuni . . . the pueblo contains seven quarters, . . . their space also contains seven quarters, and each of these seven quarters of the world is in intimate connection with a quarter of the pueblo, that is to say with a group of clans . . . Thus the social organisation has been a model for the spatial organisation and a reproduction of it. (Durkheim, 1912, p. 11)

41 Society was not simply a model which classificatory thought followed; it was its own divisions which served as divisions for the system of classification. . . . It was because men were grouped, and thought of themselves in the form of groups, that in their ideas they grouped other things. . . . (Durkheim and Mauss, 1903, p. 82)

42 It is also interesting to compare the arguments of 'The Hidden God' as a significant development of the Marxist tradition, with an example of recent thought following Durkheim, such as, for example, Mary Douglas's 'Natural Symbols' (1970).

CHAPTER 4 THE PROBLEM OF THE POWER OF KNOWLEDGE AND IDEAS

1   Marx himself attempted on a number of occasions to produce a more formally clearcut and empirically specific statement of his position; his remarks in the 'Preface to a Contribution to the Critique of Political Economy' (1962) are the most frequently quoted instance. But it is probably fair to say that he never produced anything which adequately expressed and justified the perspectives and methods of analysis so impressively deployed in his concrete historical studies. Commentators have indeed always found it easy to demonstrate major logical difficulties in Marx's abstract statements when they are literally interpreted, cf, for example Plamenatz (1963).

2   Although nothing hangs upon the point, Weber's work does give the impression that basically he was an idealist whose genuflections to the material component in history were merely part of a defensive strategy in argument.

3   Weber never sought to argue that Calvinist maxims were a sufficient cause of rational capitalism.

4   Although the argument in the main text suffices for its purpose, it could readily be supplemented at this point by a more basic criticism. There are enormous problems involved in establishing that a particular action is logically implied by a general maxim; it is possible to argue that people decide 'ex post facto' whether an action is to be considered as an implication of a general maxim or not, and then create properly logically formed accounts which display it in the manner required.

5   Consideration of the few remaining enclaves of authentic Calvinism in the modern world lends striking confirmation to the thesis.

6   This did not, however, prevent Mannheim from offering a discussion of Chiliasm as an example of the utility of the sociology of knowledge.

7   There is an analogy to be drawn here with the various ideal types of individual explicitly referred to or implicitly involved in economic theories. The various kinds of 'economic man' indicated by these theories are invariably somewhat impoverished individuals. But it would be a mistake to base criticism simply upon this neglect of important individual characteristics. It may be that certain emergent properties of monetary distribution tend systematically to reflect only a very narrow section of the social-psychological determinants of our activity, with the particular consequences of the remaining unexplicated determinants largely cancelling each other out. We may thus find, usefully encapsulated within particular concepts of 'economic man', those propensities to action, which by being systematically rather than randomly related to various monetary phenomena, assume a particular importance from the perspective defined by certain narrow economic interests. However, when these idealised conceptions are made the basis for claims about the detailed character of individuals, as does very occasionally occur, then criticism is fully deserved.

8   It might be objected that this conception is unsociological, and neglects the importance of social norms and institutions. This is not the case. Rather, the present account offers a basis upon

which an explanation of the normative component in activity can
be set. Where actors calculate upon the basis of shared knowledge,
and in the process routinely simulate the calculations of others
to take them into account in making their own, the emergence of
ordered patterns of overall activity is to be expected. The work
of the symbolic interactionists has shown very convincingly how,
on the basis of a minimum of shared interests or goals, actors
may build up a shared sense of social structure and come to act
in terms of it (cf. Rose, 1962); several of these writers do
indeed explicitly employ a calculative model of the actor (cf.
Becker, 1960, 1964). Once a sense of order is developed by interacting individuals it will become incorporated into their calculations and hence they will develop an interest in maintaining it and
in discouraging others from acting upon a different basis. On this
account of institutionalisation, the institutions which we normally,
and reasonably, treat as frameworks within which actors operate,
do not have to be set against activities as constraining, external
things; they are perce ved patterns of activity itself, treated
as data for calculatio.... That actors develop a contingent interest
in the patterns of activity they perceive, simply by calculating
on the assumption that those patterns are likely to persist for a
time, provides us with an explanation of the persistence of institutions. It is an explanation which avoids reification, and
gives rise to no surprise when we do find men changing institutional forms in response to changed needs.

9   It is important not to confuse the knowledge an actor possesses
with the verbal statements we have to use to impute such knowledge
to him. Clearly, his knowledge does not consist in a set of
particular verbal statements stored inside his head. It is useful
to employ a computer analogy and conceptualise the actor's knowledge as the programmes and memories of a programmed device. Our
verbal statements gloss such programmes and memories for the sake
of theoretical speculation. To equate an actor's knowledge with
even *his* verbal account of it may be no better than to imagine
that a computer 'thinks' in terms of 'Fortran' simply because its
inputs and outputs are intelligible in terms of that 'language'.

10 Optimistic intellectuals frequently talk as if simply by
believing in their ability to do so people could quickly arrive
at the solutions to any kind of technical problem. They see
discourse which acknowledges the existence of any limitations upon
the possibility of thought as ideologically determined. On the
other hand, those who have actually worked to extend our stock of
instrumentally applicable knowledge tend to take a different view.

11 This view is in direct contradiction to current so-called
Marxist analyses, which regard particular legitimations of current
social arrangements as crucial to their survival. However, belief
in the potency of mere ideas is probably a harmless delusion for
political activists. In their self-defined task of spreading the
'correct' ideas through the working class they do indeed have the
kind of effect they desire. Not by implanting particular ideas,
but by stimulating organisation and the creation of institutional
forms. It is precisely through the construction and perfection of
forms of organisation over the long term that the power of the
lower classes in industrial societies has so successfully been
increased.

12   Examples can be found in many standard works in the history
of science; but for readily intelligible materials cf. Rudwick
(1972); and for an explicitly sociological discussion Barnes
(1974).
13   The technical and conceptual problems involved in the attempt
to state how cultural change would have proceeded in the absence
of some particular material cause are formidable.
14   The use of a cultural resource in the successful generation of
new knowledge must be treated as unpredictable as a specific event,
since to check that the resource is so utilisable is essentially
the same thing as to use it successfully, i.e. as to make the
innovation itself.
15   In what follows, Marx's distinction between 'base' and 'superstructure' is considered only in so far as it relates to a distinction between instrumentally applicable knowledge and rationalisations.   Its further interesting implications concerning the
causal relationships between various areas within the field of
'conscious human activity' itself are not considered, even though
they are of great relevance to the sociology of knowledge.
16   It is worth noting here how the key difficulty in solving,
say, a mathematical problem, is not that of remembering forms of
solution, but that of seeing the problem as a particular sort of
problem, generally by recognising an analogy between it and a
familiar concrete problem which one already knows how to solve.
There should be no need to apologise for a concrete form of exposition of explanatory procedures.
17   As far as Marx himself is concerned I have never had difficulty
in reading him as a thoroughly naturalistic thinker.   A cogent case
for such an interpretation has been made by Jordan (1967), although
the discussion of dialectical materialism with which this book is
mainly concerned is not so satisfactory.

BIBLIOGRAPHY

AVINERI, S. (1968), 'The Social and Political Thought of Karl Marx', Cambridge University Press.

BARNES, S. B. (1974), 'Scientific Knowledge and Sociological Theory', Routledge & Kegan Paul, London.

BARNES, S. B. (1976), Natural rationality: a neglected concept in the social sciences, 'Phil. Soc. Sci.', vol. 6, no. 2, pp. 115-26.

BARNES, S. B. and LAW, J. (1976), Whatever should be done with indexical expressions?, 'Theory and Society', vol. 3, no. 2, pp. 223-37.

BECKER, H. S. (1960), Notes on the concept of commitment, 'A.J.S.', 66, pp. 32-40.

BECKER, H. S. (1964), Personal change in adult life, 'Sociometry', vol. 27, pp. 40-53.

BHASKAR, R. (1975), 'A Realist Theory of Science', Leeds Books, Leeds.

BLOOR, D. (1973), Wittgenstein and Mannheim on the sociology of mathematics, 'Stud. Hist. Phil. Sci.', vol. 4, no. 2, pp. 173-91.

BLOOR, D. (1976), 'Knowledge and Social Imagery', Routledge & Kegan Paul, London.

BURNS, T. (ed.) (1969), 'Industrial Man', Penguin, Harmondsworth.

CHILD, A. (1941), The problem of imputation in the sociology of knowledge, 'Ethics', vol. 51, no. 2, pp. 200-19.

CHILD, A. (1944), The problem of imputation resolved, 'Ethics', vol. 51, no. 1, pp. 96-109.

COLEMAN, W. (1970), Bateson and chromosomes: conservative thought in science, 'Centaurus', vol. 15, pp. 228-314.

CURTIS, J. E. and PETRAS, J. W. (eds) (1970), 'The Sociology of Knowledge', Duckworth, London.

DOUGLAS, J. D. (ed.) (1970), 'Understanding Everyday Life', Routledge & Kegan Paul, London.

DOUGLAS, M. (1966), 'Purity and Danger', Routledge & Kegan Paul, London.

DOUGLAS, M. (1970), Natural Symbols', Barrie & Jenkins, London.

DURKHEIM, E. (1912), 'Elementary Forms of Religious Life', Eng. trans. (1961), Free Press, New York.

DURKHEIM, E. and MAUSS, M. (1903), 'Primitive Classification', Eng. trans. (1963), Cohen & West, London.

ELIAS, N. (1971), Sociology of knowledge - new perspectives, 'Sociology', vol. 5, no. 2, pp. 149 ff.; no. 3, pp. 368 ff.
FEUER, L. S. (1975), 'Ideology and the Ideologists', Blackwell, Oxford.
FORDER, H. G. (1927), 'Euclidean Geometry', Cambridge University Press.
FORMAN, P. (1971), Weimar culture, causality and the quantum theory, 'Hist. Stud. Phys. Sci.', vol. 3, pp. 1-115.
GASMAN, D. (1971), 'The Scientific Origins of National Socialism', Elsevier, New York.
GOLDMANN, L. (1964), 'The Hidden God', Eng. trans. Thody, Routledge & Kegan Paul, London.
GOMBRICH, E. H. (1959), 'Art and Illusion', Phaidon, London.
HABERMAS, J. (1972), 'Knowledge and Human Interests', Heinemann, London.
HABERMAS, J. (1973), A postscript to 'Knowledge and human interests', trans. Lenhardt, 'Phil. Soc. Sci.', vol. 3, pp. 97-115.
HALÉVY, E. (1928), 'The Growth of Philosophical Radicalism', Eng. trans. Morris, Faber, London.
HALLER, J. S. (1971), 'Outcasts from Evolution', Illinois University Press, Chicago.
HARWOOD, J. (1976-7), The race - intelligence controversy: a socio-logical approach, Pts 1 and 2, 'Social Studies of Science, vols 6 and 7, pp. 89-104.
HEATH, T. L. (1925), 'The Thirteen Books of Euclid's Elements', Cambridge University Press.
HESSE, M. (1972), In defence of objectivity, 'Proc. Brit. Acad.', vol. 58, pp. 3-20.
HESSE, M. (1974), 'The Structure of Scientific Inference', Macmillan, London.
HORTON, R. and FINNEGAN, R. (eds) (1973), 'Modes of Thought', Faber, London.
HUACO, G. A. (1971), On ideology, 'Acta Sociologica', vol. 14, pp. 245-55.
IVINS, W. M. (1953), 'Prints and Visual Communication', Harvard University Press, Cambridge, Mass.
JORDAN, Z. A. (1967), 'The Evolution of Dialectical Materialism', Macmillan, New York.
KUHN, T. S. (1970), 'The Structure of Scientific Revolutions', 2nd edition, University of Chicago Press.
LAKATOS, I. (1963), Proofs and refutations, 'Brit, J. Phil. Sci.', vol. 14, pp. 1-25, 120-39, 221-45, 296-342.
LEVI-STRAUSS, C. (1962), 'Totemism', Eng trans. (1969), Penguin, Harmondsworth.
LUKÁCS, G. (1923), 'Geschichte und Klassenbewurstsein', translated in English and published as 'History and Class-Consciousness' (1971), Merlin Press, London.
LUKES, S. (1974), Relativism: cognitive and moral, 'Arist. Soc. Sup.', vol. 48, pp. 165-89.
MACKENZIE, D. A. (1976), Eugenics in Britain, 'Social Studies in Science', vol. 3, nos 3-4, pp. 219 ff.
MACKENZIE, D. A. and BARNES, S. B. (1975), Biometrician v Mendelian: a controversy and its explanation, 'Kölner Zeitschrift für Soziologie', special issue, vol. 18, pp. 165-96.

MANNHEIM, K. (1936), 'Ideology and Utopia', trans, L. Wirth and
E. Shils, Routledge & Kegan Paul, London.
MANNHEIM, K. (1953), Conservative thought in 'Essays in Sociology
and Social Psychology', Routledge & Kegan Paul, London.
MARX, K. (1962), 'Preface to A Contribution to the Critique of
Political Economy', pp. 361-5 of 'Marx and Engels: Selected Works',
Foreign Language Press, Moscow.
MARX, K. (1969), 'Theories of Surplus Value, Parts I, II, III',
Lawrence & Wishart, London.
MARX, K. and ENGELS, F. (1970), 'The German Ideology', Part 1,
C. J. Arthur (ed.), Lawrence & Wishart, London.
PLAMENATZ, J. (1963), 'Man and Society, Vol. 2', Longmans, London.
POLANYI, M. (1958), 'Personal Knowledge', Routledge & Kegan Paul,
London.
POPPER, K. R. (1934), 'Logik der Forschung', Vienna.
RAVETZ, J. R. (1971), 'Scientific Knowledge and Its Social Problems',
Oxford University Press, London.
ROSE, A. M. (ed.) (1962), 'Human Behaviour and Social Processes',
Routledge & Kegan Paul, London.
RUDWICK, M. J. S. (1972), 'The Meaning of Fossils. Episodes in the
History of Palaentology', MacDonald, London.
RUDWICK, M. J. S. (1976), The emergence of a visual language for
geological science, 1760-1840, 'History of Science', vol. 14,
pt 3, no. 25, pp. 149-95.
SHAPIN, S. and BARNES, S. B. (1977), Science, nature and control:
interpreting Mechanics' Institutes, 'Social Studies of Science',
vol. 7, no. 1.
THOMPSON, E. P. (1963), 'The Making of the English Working Class',
Gollancz, London.
TOULMIN, S. (1953), 'The Philosophy of Science', Hutchinson,
London.
TREVOR-ROPER, H. R. (1967), 'Religion, the Reformation and Social
Change', Macmillan, London.
WEBER, M. (1930), 'The Protestant Ethic and the Spirit of
Capitalism', trans. T. Parsons, Unwin, London.
WILSON, B. (ed.) (1971), 'Rationality', Blackwell, Oxford.

INDEX